TRUST
the
FORCE

TRUST
the
FORCE

Change Your Life
Through Attitudinal Healing

TODD DAVISON, M.D.

JASON ARONSON INC.
Northvale, New Jersey
London

Portions from *A Course in Miracles* ® © 1975, reprinted by permission of the Foundation for Inner Peace, Inc. P.O. Box 598, Mill Valley, CA 94942.

This book was set in 11 pt. New Century Schoolbook by Alpha Graphics of Pittsfield, New Hampshire, and printed and bound by Book-mart of North Bergen, New Jersey.

10 9 8 7 6 5 4 3 2

Library of Congress Cataloging-in-Publication Data

Davison, Todd.
    Trust the force : change your life through attitudinal healing / by Todd Davison.
       p. cm.
    Includes bibliographical references and index.
    ISBN 1-56821-594-0
    1. Self-actualization (Psychology) 2. Diaries—Authorship—
Psychological aspects. 3. Meditation. 4. Attitude change.
5. Course in miracles. I. Title.
BF637.S4D38 1995
158'.1—dc20   95-18420

Manufactured in the United States of America. Jason Aronson Inc. offers books and cassettes. For information and catalog write to Jason Aronson Inc., 230 Livingston Street, Northvale, New Jersey 07647.

Contents

Part II: Meditation Exercises   **41**

WEEK 1   **43**

Things Are Not the Way I See Them Now: Perception, Preferences, and Their Limitations

WEEK 2   77

Emotions May Be Viewed as either Love or Fear

Acknowledgments

There are many people who have supported me in writing this book and in my work in Attitudinal Healing. My most important teacher is my wife Renée. She read every word and encouraged me throughout this process and throughout my life. She uses Attitudinal Healing with me every day. I cannot thank her enough for her support. My sons, Michael and Jeffrey, have also been my teachers. My sister Barbara is a constant source of inspiration because she is one of the most positive people I know. My parents were most important teachers, as were my grandparents. My Aunt Betty shows me how important this moment is in life every time I speak to her.

Susan Deutsch, my office manager for the past decade, practices these principles, attends our Monday noon group, facilitates another group and instills in our office staff the heart of this practice. Paul Gray, my teacher, psychoanalyst, and friend showed me the way my story impacts my daily life. Christine Nuernberg and Ruth Holst read the first draft of this book and critiqued it so thoroughly that I began to take it seriously myself.

Curtis Bristol and Bud Pray have studied with me weekly for the last twelve years to learn ways to make psychoanalysis more useful to our patients. They reviewed the theory in this book and their sharp observations allowed me to rethink many theoretical positions.

John Schuler, president of Columbia Health Systems, supported the institution of Attitudinal Healing in the Behavioral Medicine Center at Columbia Hospital. It took courage to allow a new approach and he never wavered in his support, without which this entire endeavor would not have been possible.

Steve Steury showed me how to stay calm in meetings. Betty Huse, David Leach, Jon Meyer, and David Black have also been important teachers to me.

Jerry Jampolski guided me through the process of getting this book published. He was available to me by telephone for coaching whenever I needed him. Carolyn Washburne edited this book going over every line, every word, and every syllable. It is hard to find anyone who will give so much attention to detail. In addition she lent me her friends who had been through this process and they provided useful advice and guidance.

All members of our study groups worked with these lessons and taught me how to use them, especially Bob and Carol Gresk, David Clowers and Juliet Hale Hills who have been such a help. Caryl Zaar, our in-patient nurse manager co-facilitates groups with me and brings a glow of healing wherever she goes.

Tom Kopka taught me how to meditate. He teaches meditation classes for all comers every two months. He lives these principles and is the heart of our employees' assistance program at Columbia.

Joan Metzler, the manager of Behavioral Medicine, found a way to make Attitudinal Healing Groups, which are offered free to our patients, fiscally possible. She also co-facilitates groups and leads stress management seminars using Attitudinal Healing.

JoAnn Hankwitz, Colleen Flores, and Terri Koch facilitate groups and use Attitudinal Healing in individual therapy in our psychotherapy clinic. Debbie Rupp, office manager of Behavioral Medicine, attends our groups and uses the principles wherever she goes. Jo Ann Timmerman uses Attitudinal Healing in our day hospital program. Jann McClintock found *A Course in Miracles®* for me and helped me start the process. Jo Sims works with patients using the same principles.

Michael Moskowitz of Jason Aronson Inc. maintained an enthusiasm for this project from the first time I talked to him about it. What a gift!

David Holloway encouraged me to get through the first ninety lessons in *A Course in Miracles*. After that it began to fall into place.

The medical staff of Columbia Hospital may have thought what we were doing in Behavioral Medicine was unusual at times, but they were quietly supportive and sent their patients.

I feel indebted to John Lehrmann and all the residents in Harry Prosen's psychiatry residency at the Medical College of Wisconsin who showed an interest in Attitudinal Healing. Carl Chan, director of residency training, has also been supportive.

Sam and Sarah gave me "Two Dog Meditation," the most relaxing experience imaginable. They infused me with their enthusiasm for the meditation process and protected me from unwanted intruders including invisible militant microbes that only dogs can see.

Preface

1. WHAT'S LOVE GOT TO DO WITH IT?

Trust the Force is an introduction to applied spiritual healing using psychoanalytic principles as its basis. The term spiritual healing may raise the eyebrows of those who consider themselves scientific. They may ask questions such as the following:

1. If spirituality has a positive effect on physical and mental processes how is that effect different from a psychological one?

2. If spiritual healing is an energic phenomena how is that energy spiritual rather than biological or chemical energy?

3. Why is love an essential component of spiritual healing?

These are excellent questions. The first question's answer seems clear to me. Any effect may be understood from more than one perspective. Psychological effects may be understood from a biological perspective and vice versa.

For instance, psychiatrists have known for ages that a positive relationship with a patient is an important determinant of how well an antidepressant will work with that patient. From a psychological perspective the prescription of a medication may have many significant meanings for patients. One is an implicit promise that while they may feel alone in many aspects of their life, in those areas concerning their depression, the physician will be with them. They carry a promise of that in the prescription itself. How many times have psychiatrists heard that patients' sleep disturbances cleared when they had pills in their medicine cabinet without ingesting any medication at all? A second psychological effect is a reassurance that someone can understand their problem. They are not beyond normal human experience, and a third factor in prescribing a medication is that there is hope.

From a spiritual perspective, in prescribing an antidepressant, one might describe all those effects as fulfilling a eucharistic function, that is, my agent is with you to heal your suffering. Wherever you go my agent will be with you representing me. So, you are not alone in this suffering. You may be alone in other aspects of your life but when it comes to this depression, wherever you go I am with you.

The ability to describe one effect from many different points of view is inherent in human experience.

The answer to the second question is similar to the first. Healing may be described as an energic phenomenon and that energy will be a function of the theory from which your description springs. In other words, no description is theory free. One might describe a recovery from depression from a biological perspective as a replenishing of the patient's serotonin, norepinephrine and other neurotransmitter substances, or from a psychological point of view as a translation of superego energy into ego energy, or from a spiritual perspective as bringing love back into the heart.

The third question, "What does love have to do with it?" seems to beg for a theory. What are the options? Let us assume that Freud was right. Man has two driving forces: libido and aggression. Libido fuels sexual pleasure, respect, honor, compassion, and noticing similarities. These various phenomena are lumped in common parlance under the word "love."

Aggression fuels fight, flight, disdain, domination, depression, guilt, shame, and noticing distinctions and dissimilarities. If healing is a process of joining, it is fueled by libido. Aggression does not go away. If properly balanced by libido it fuels learning, seeking knowledge and other seeking behaviors. The expression of libido that we can experience is love, which in healing is used as an inclusive term to stand for respect, honor, and compassion. The problem with love is that the term also carries a sexual connotation that leads to concerns about abuse. Sexual abuse is a serious problem in mental health and religious practice. Yet sexual feelings are a normal part of our day-to-day experience. How can we guard against abuse?

In the following lessons we will learn how to honor our feelings without putting all of them into action. Stepping back from our immediate experience and choosing carefully how we act is one of the most important aspects of Attitudinal Healing.

2. WILL THIS BOOK HELP ME ANSWER THE BIG QUESTION: WHY AM I HERE AND WHAT'S LIFE ALL ABOUT?

More than anything I hope that this book will give you an opportunity to learn how to access a part of your self that will help you find that answer. Here is what I think about that subject:

According to some cosmologists all matter began as a single point in the big bang. Since each of us is matter, we are each predestined to occupy a certain coordinate on the time–space continuum. Each of us has choices that will influence the rest of time and space. Among the most important choices we can make are choices of our attitudes.

What makes attitude so important is that attitude dictates our experiences. Three of the most important attitudes to me are the following: (1) all emotions are good, (2) all troubles contain a lesson for us to learn, and (3) we live best in the present because it is the only time we can make choices. If we live in the present, shame and guilt are minimized because they are in the past. Yet shame and guilt are good because they tell when we are not living in the present. They can be markers of healing work to do. If we feel anxiety, we are anticipating the future. Anxiety can be used as a marker for healing work to do. If we pay attention to the messages of anxiety, guilt, and shame, we will see them as helping us focus our healing work by presenting us with opportunities for learning.

We have two things of real value: love and our experiences. It is amazing how we search for something that we can count on in life. We search for something that will continue to nurture us when we have the sources of unending peace already within us. The more we give away love and our experiences the more we get in return. In this book I hope to share with you my love and my experiences. I hope you will share your experiences with me as well. If we share with each other we will move toward experiencing healthy interdependence, which may be our best chance for spreading peace.

Part I
Introduction:
Trust the Force

Do you remember the scene in the film, *Star Wars,* when Luke Skywalker flies down a canyon in the Death Star space ship on his way to delivering a warhead to a ventilation shaft? The way I remember that scene, Luke tries to find the shaft in his video range finder but he can't lock on the target. He gets frustrated. Just then the voice of Obie Wan Kanobie intones, "Trust the force, Luke." Luke obeys by swinging the electronic video sight away and accomplishing instinctively what he was unable to do with modern technology. He delivers the torpedo to the target by trusting a force inside himself, a force he can get in touch with when he is able to calm the distortions of his senses.

Re-viewing the film recently, I discovered that this scene is not there the way I'd remembered it. My memory had synthesized several scenes in the movie to fit my wishes. I wanted a clear statement in the film about people's internal homing mechanism that, once discovered, is of greater value than telescopes, radar, or computerized, video, lock-in devices. The scene I remember would have been a perfect opportunity to make such a statement.

That is the way memory works. It remembers things the way I want to remember them. In this case, my wish was to find support for trusting a force inside me. I want, as Luke Skywalker had in my memory, a force that will guide me to find practical solutions to everyday problems and move me toward rewarding goals. Not only do I want this but so do many people. In fact, one goal of psychoanalysis, psychotherapy, stress reduction, and meditation is to be able to trust a force inside ourselves, a force of inspired, reasoned intuition. To be able to trust this force is the most reassuring capacity we can enjoy. Imagine believing that no matter what challenge life brings us, we can find a way to be at peace with it. What a gift! We all have the capacity to trust the force. There are many roads to this capacity, but they all take some study and practice.

MINUTES A DAY CAN CHANGE YOUR LIFE

This course is designed to change your life in a relatively short period of time. If you spend thirty minutes reading and meditating in the morning and a few minutes reflecting and writing in the evening you can achieve peace of mind. The course is eight weeks long. If you repeat the lessons three times in twenty-four weeks they will be with you forever. They will be indelibly etched in your unconscious mind, which will apply them automatically when-ever you need them. This course includes three proven self-help methods: Attitudinal Healing, meditation practice, and journaling.

ATTITUDINAL HEALING

Attitudinal Healing[1] is shifting perception from an unpeaceful state to a way of looking at things that permits peace of mind. It can be achieved by applying the principles found in *A Course in Miracles*®.[2] None of the principles in that system is new. They can be found in the works of many great thinkers, from Epicurus to Buddha to Sigmund Freud. All of the principles suggest reshaping our attitudes in the direction of peacefulness. These principles are a distillation of wisdom proven by the test of time, principles that work to improve the quality of life. The seven elements of Attitudinal Healing begin on p. 6. They are called elements because they are fundamental. There may be more than seven elements but there are no fewer than these.

MEDITATION PRACTICE

Meditation is sitting quietly, with my eyes closed, in a comfortable erect posture and breathing through my nose if that feels comfortable. I notice my abdomen rise with the in-breath and fall with the out-breath. When other thoughts intrude, I am aware of them but do not judge. I gently move my attention back to my abdomen as it moves in and out with my breath. Following my breath is following the rise and fall of my abdomen.

Meditation is useful because it slows all the systems in my body and gives me a chance to observe mind and body. Also, it serves as a platform to launch the lessons. One way to combine a lesson with breathing during meditation is to think of the first half of the lesson on the in-breath and the second half of the meditation on the out-breath. Here is an example from Lesson 34 of *A Course in Miracles*®: IN, *I can see peace*, OUT, *instead of this.*[3] Repeat the process three to five times at the beginning. Then either follow your thoughts, feelings, and bodily sensations wherever they go or, return to thinking about the rise and fall of your abdomen, *in* and *out*. Then, at the end of meditation over three to five breath cycles, repeat the lesson again.

Any length of time is useful for meditation, from one minute to one hour. Each person has a different optimal time. Try different periods like 10, 15, 20, or 30 minutes to find out which one is best for you. You will know when you find the optimal length of time. Trust the force.

At first, in formal meditation practice, it is best to follow the breath. As I breathe in, I think to myself, "In." As I breathe out, I think, "Out." As I do this, other thoughts, emotions, and bodily sensations come to mind. As soon as I am aware of them, I label them without judging: "Plan," "Memory," "Fantasy," "To-do list," "Anger," "Itch." Then I return to my abdomen, "In" and "Out." When I refocus on my breath, I do so with gentleness. I kindly and gently usher myself back to my breath.

Practice, in this context, simply means doing as opposed to preparing for something or improving something.

Formal meditation means meditation done in a particular way, such as sitting. Once I have experience in formal meditation, I may find that I can enter a relaxed state, fully aware of the present with my eyes open, any time I choose.

There are useful subjects of attention other than my breath, such as bodily sensations, thoughts, and emotions. Instead of returning to my breath as soon as I become aware of other subjects, I may choose to follow my bodily sensations by just noticing them. I may notice thoughts and emotions the same way. When I face these sensations, thoughts, and emotions without judging them; without using them as planned action; and without being moved to act as they come to mind, I optimize formal meditation practice. By doing this, I learn to be at peace rather than scurrying around with a sense of urgency. The Swiss psychologist, Carl Jung, wrote, "Hurry is not of the devil, it is the devil." Hurry is definitely the opposite of enjoying what is available to savor at the moment, whether we label it "the devil" or not.

At times, sitting is not comfortable for meditation; and then lying, walking, or exercising may be used for meditation. When walking and exercising, I may choose to focus on a repetitive motion, rather than the rise and fall of my abdomen.

In all meditation practice the idea is to let the mind be still and calm. Many natural analogies come to mind such as a still pool of water or a calm lake. But no matter how peaceful the analogy, there are moments when it is very difficult to calm the mind and then additional measures can be useful. One of the most useful methods for calming a restless mind is repeating soundlessly, a simple, two-syllable, nonsense word. When following my breath is not calming, saying over and over to myself, "trutfoe," or any other two-syllable word, may bring a deeper peace by calming the nagging inner voices. Sometimes counting the out-breaths serves a similar purpose.

JOURNALING

I choose to write in my journal at the end of the day. I write down one example of using the day's lesson to achieve a moment of healing, a shift of perception that has helped me experience peace of mind that day. In a separate section of my journal I write down any major disruptions to my peace of mind, that is, times when my fearfulness lasted for more than a few minutes or an hour. All of these methods are used to apply the seven elements of Attitudinal Healing.

SEVEN ELEMENTS
OF ATTITUDINAL HEALING

1. Things are not the way I see them now.[4]
2. Emotions may be viewed as either love or fear.[5]
3. My childhood story distorts my adult experience.
4. Forgiveness paves the road to peace.[6]
5. Healing is my choice to make.[7]
6. Learning is a key to a better life. Teaching is a good way to learn.[8]
7. I have an inner guide, the force, which I can access in quiet moments.[9]

1. Things are not the way I see them now.[10]

My perceptions are amazingly inaccurate and limited. My sight, hearing, and other senses are remarkably biased. Physicists tells us that we apprehend only one part in a billion of the world around us. Many psychology experiments have shown that we often do not know, literally, what we have seen or heard. For example, I clearly did not know what I had heard in the Luke Skywalker scene previously mentioned.

We already know of many instances when we must not trust our senses. For example, our senses tell us the world is flat. We do not believe that because we have learned that the apparent flatness is an illusion determined by our limited line of sight. Our senses tell us the sun rises in the East and sets in the West. We do not believe that because we know it is an illusion based on our inability to feel the Earth rotate. It is our planet rotating not the sun moving. Our sight tells us that grass is green, but we know that perception has more to do with the rods and cones in our eyes than anything else. Bats and dogs, for example, probably see very different colors.

Our senses tell us that we are the center of all experience. We try not to believe that, but it becomes more complex because experiencing ourselves as the center of the universe is ongoing and unending. It is hard to write one full page without saying something that another person can barely understand because she is not inside my head. It is hard to live one hour in which I do not ask something of someone that he could not possibly understand because he is not inside my mind.

Typically I might ask, "Renée, have you seen my blue thing?" This has become a joke in my family. My wife,

Renée, replies, "Oh your blue thing, let's see, is it animal, vegetable, or mineral?" I expect, only for a moment, that Renée will know that I am looking for the blue pants to my warm-up suit. There is no way she could know this, but for a moment I expect her to. That is a sign of the egocentric illusion. That is, I experience myself as the center of the universe and everyone around me must know what I mean without my needing to give sufficient information to make myself understood. This illusion is based on a belief grounded in my senses. Since I see the world only with *my* eyes, feel it only with *my* touch, smell it only with *my* nose, and hear it only with *my* ears, then *my* experience must be central. The more insecure I feel, the more I believe in my egocentric illusion. One mark of a frightened person is *certainty* about his perceptions and as the old saying goes, "Never in doubt, but frequently wrong."

My senses tell me that I am separate from you. But if I were able to see on a subatomic level, I might see that you and I are exchanging atoms each time I exhale and you inhale or each time you exhale and I inhale. From a distance our separateness also might be challenged if I were to see you and me interact in a way very similar to everyone else on this planet. From a distance we might appear to be a part of a much bigger picture of interaction that looks like a carefully choreographed ballet. That is what is meant by at-one-ment. We are one. We cooperate and we depend on each other in ways that are still hard to imagine.

An excellent example of cooperation and dependency among people is found in a simple yellow pencil, the kind we used in class as kids. Milton Friedman told this story on the "Booknotes" television program. Do you know that not one person in the world can make a pencil? It's a fact. No one in the world can make a pencil from start to finish. In order to make a pencil, someone in Wisconsin must know how to cut down a tree and send it to the mill in Appleton. There are people at the mill who know how to saw that tree into just the right dimensions for the pencil. Simultaneously, workers in Central America are mining graphite, sending it to a mill to be made into just the right form to be inserted into the wood. In Pittsburgh other people are pouring steel to make the eraser holder. In Malaysia workers are tapping rubber trees that are not even native to the land but were brought there years ago by botanists. The Malaysians have started the process of making the eraser, and somewhere in upstate New York other workers put the whole thing together. All of these people work independently and cooperatively to bring me the pencil that I depend upon to mark corrections in this text. That is a small example of how we depend on so many people working together everyday.

At-one-ment means that I am similar to every other living thing, and probably not that different at a chemical level from the things I call inanimate. When I accept at-one-ment, I emphasize similarities rather than differences designed to make me feel superior or set apart. When I let myself feel at one with another, fear disappears.

A special way to feel this at-one-ment is the use of bright light meditation. Here is how it works. After my formal meditation practice, where I attempt to limit my attention as much as possible to my breath, I imagine a warm bright light in the middle of my body. I hold that image of light until I can feel the warmth. Then I let the warmth spread all over my body. When I feel ready, I let it spread out of me and to those people and things in my

surroundings and even those people in my past with whom
I wish to feel a connection. I imagine that warmth spreading out of my body to them. The color of the light depends
on the day or my feelings, but two characteristics are
always there: it is warm and it is bright. In the moments
when I feel this warmth, all kinds of ideas come to me
about how much I depend on others. I feel that interde-
pendency and marvel at it.

2. Emotions may be viewed as either love or fear.[11]

In early psychoanalytic theory Sigmund Freud said that
there is only one driving psychological force, the sexual
one, which he called libido. According to Freud, libido fuels
both love and its desexualized components, respect and
compassion. When a child is thwarted in receiving the love
he wants, he becomes aggressive. Aggression is seen as a
result of the child's fear that she cannot have her loving
wishes gratified.

This is a productive way to think about the two drives;
either I feel love or fear. When I act irritably, I am frightened and calling out for kindness and compassion. When
I extend compassion to an angry person, I am choosing
joining rather than separation. I am making a decision not
to believe what my senses tell me, that is, we are separate, and instead to believe what I know to be true, that
is, we are one. If we are one, when I extend myself in compassion to you, I help myself.

Another angle on this is to divide my experience between my two selves: a frightened-self and a loving-self.
My frightened-self began in childhood when I feared I

would not get my loving wishes gratified, so I decided to act tough instead. My frightened-self believes in a world of scarcity. "There is only so much stuff and I must get my share and hopefully a little bit more." It tells me that I have to look out for myself and get all that I can, and it shouts, "gimme, gimme." It glorifies temporal things such as my body, alcohol, drugs, failure, guilt, depression, shame, material possessions, and money.

When I am operating from my frightened-self, I make fun of attempts to explore an inner world. I believe that love is a futile whimpering of frailty. I say, "No pain, no gain." I want to drive a hard bargain and walk over other people to get ahead. I believe that anger and fear are not only inevitable, but that those emotions are justified and reasonable. In my fearfulness I attack first and ask questions later.

My frightened-self began in childhood when I sought to prove that I could act big even though I was small. It began when I was frustrated over not getting all the love I wanted and decided that my problems must have come from my badness. In order to have that badness offset, I needed something from someone else. Unable to tolerate the idea of my badness I put the badness outside myself onto others. It was others' badness that caused me trouble. In other words it all began with my own sense of guilt that I dealt with by projecting onto others.

Over the years my frightened-self had a lot to say about relationships. It said that "me first" was the way to go. I should insist on "me first" even though it leads to feelings of alienation from others. When I am operating from my frightened-self, I want instantaneous gratification, with sexual gratification and physical pleasure at the top of the list. I brook no criticism. I insist on being obeyed no matter what, and despite unlimited selfishness, I expect to be admired, even adored.

My frightened-self's standard is a double standard. While it is all right for me to *act* small-minded, mean, manipulative, envious, and jealous, it is not all right for you even to *have those feelings*. If you do have them and show them, even for an instant, then it is a sign that you are not the slave I want you to be.

When I am operating from my frightened-self, I am ever vigilant for enemies or those who, even accidently, might operate at cross purposes to mine. "When in doubt, pout!" is my rallying cry. No slight is too small not to make a federal case of it. After all, I believe that "Hate is a more important emotion than love, because without hate, vengeance means nothing."

My frightened-self believes in special relationships. *A Course in Miracles*® defines special relationships as those onto which we project guilt.[12] There are two types of special relationships: special hate relationships and special love relationships. Special hate relationships develop scapegoats. In a scapegoat relationship I persuade myself and sometimes others that one person is responsible for all the troubles. Then I ostracize that person. Special love relationships are merely thinly disguised hate relationships. In a special love relationship I decide that you are the only person for me. You are the only person who can offset my sense of badness. Then I make a deal that you will act the way I want you to in order to fulfill my desires (my script for you) and I will do the same for you (your script for me). Scripts are the particular ways we want others to behave. Since neither of us can really follow each other's script, we ultimately fail each other.

Bring in the goat. I blame you for the failure because you did not live up to your end of the bargain. Then I ostracize you.

When I operate from this defensive posture, I am afraid. I cannot help being frightened; it is a part of life. In this respect my frightened-self is not bad, it is just operating on limited information. It was formed, after all, when I was a wee little tyke living in the land of the giants. When my needs were not met, or when I was brushed aside, these giants seemed pretty mean and dangerous. They became even more dangerous when I projected my anger onto them and experienced myself on the receiving end of my own projected rage.

Now when I experience others as dangerous, I can recognize this as a moment of reliving a childhood experience in the land of the giants. This experience is partially a fiction full of blame that I made up to explain my painful feelings. I can reduce the time I spend in fear by recognizing some of my options as an adult. One option is to adopt a belief system different from the one my frightened-self is selling. Remember, the frightened-self grows out of the fear that I cannot have my loving wishes gratified. There were times when that was true in the land of the giants. What if I believe that is not so true anymore? Then an alternative belief system would be available to me. That alternative is the belief system of my loving-self, in other words, the force.

My loving-self is fueled by the force. The force is love and love is my essence. If the frightened-self developed out of fear that I could not have my loving feelings gratified, then when I realize that I am much less easy to thwart as an adult, I can be more hopeful about reaping the benefits of loving feelings. In the belief system of my loving-self the purpose of relationships is to join with the essence of others through the extension of caring and compassion. When I am compassionate, I focus on similarities rather than on differences. I see relationships as opportunities for giving, learning, and growth. When I operate from the force, the goal of life is inner peace. I attain peace of mind by seeing myself more clearly through introspection. When I operate from the force, things that I hate in myself when I operate from my frightened-self are merely errors to be corrected, not transgressions to be remembered and paid for indefinitely with guilt and shame.

The act of healing is an act of compassion. Whether I show compassion for myself when I am frightened and irritable, or for my friend who is frightened and acting like a jerk, the act of healing requires forgiveness and joining. I, no matter how irritable, am connected to the force where I can find forgiveness and calming. Others, no matter how mean they may seem when they are frightened, are connected to me through their essence. In Attitudinal Healing forgiveness is my function. I ask myself to be a love finder rather than a fault finder. This is not a stance of capitulation, it is a stance of maximizing options without getting stuck in a reactive mode.

In the exercises that follow *I do **not** ask myself to ignore any feelings*. With a compassionate center, allowing myself to feel anger, hate, depression, shame, and blame may be the initial step in healing because such feelings help me identify *where* renewal is needed. There is no surer way to perpetuate misery than to attempt to avoid feelings. Feelings are not my problem. It is the attempts to avoid feelings that cause me misery. Feelings are not pathological; however it is my quest for actions or things to offset my feelings that are my downfall. If I try to find clothes that make me feel taller I will ultimately fail. If I involve myself in action to keep busy and not feel bored, I will find that I have to slow down some time. And, when I do, I will still have the feelings that I've attempted to avoid. If I try to drown my feelings in alcohol, tranquilizers, antidepressants, or anything else, I will ultimately find that the feelings are still there. Medications can be used to moderate feelings while I am learning to face them, but medications are only adjuncts, not answers.

A rule to follow is "*No strong feeling originates in adulthood.*" So all strong feelings are good because they may be used as beacons that lead me to heal myself in the present as well as in childhood. Beacons are to be celebrated, not repressed or ignored. Strong feelings of hate, hurt, shame, and guilt may be embraced as useful aspects of myself that light the way to introspective work.

With introspection, the same aggressive energy that fuels anger may be loosed from past bonds to fuel useful mastery in my life, today. If I can see where my anger is stuck and loosen it through forgiveness, I can achieve a moment of healing. In my meditations I can trace the origins of those feelings and let them lead me to forgive my parents, siblings, and others who disrupted my peacefulness in the past. This aggressive energy, once stuck in the past, may be freed to see more clearly.

My loving-self is slow to react. My frightened-self speaks first. When I react, I react from my frightened-self. When I respond, I respond from my loving-self, the force. The only way to get in touch with the force is to quiet my senses and be receptive to my experience of calm, quiet inspiration. With some practice I can shorten the time it takes to receive guidance, but it still takes time. Counting to ten as a way to deal with a perceived injustice is an attempt to gain time to access inner wisdom. Another way is to be still for a few moments, follow my breath until my frightened-self quiets down, and then to pay attention for compassionate guidance. In the quiet I can begin to experience my inner wisdom, the force.

There is a road of love and a road of fear. Which one we follow is our choice. The road of love is the road less traveled. In an instant I make my choice. In this instant. This special instant is all the time there is. In this moment I have everything I want. The past is gone, and the future is not yet here. Since there is no time but now, I have everything I need. I can enter this special instant any time I wish just by focusing on my breath. This special instant is a gift. That is why it is called the present.

3. My childhood story distorts my adult experience.

We all have a unique set of emotional characteristics that we attribute to other people. When we transfer these emotional attributes from our childhood story onto others in our everyday life, we feel on the receiving end of aggression and tyranny. We know we are reexperiencing our childhood story when we believe that someone is more guilty than we are and therefore we, as the less guilty, are owed something by the more guilty one. The emotional characteristics we attribute to the villains and ogres in our everyday life come from the way we experienced gigantic and important people through our child's mind and child's eyes. We reinvent the people in our childhood drama over and over again in our adult lives. We reinvent past, troubling relationships until we learn to heal them.

One way to think of this is that our stories are doors to discovering the lessons we have yet to learn.

My friend, Joe, for example, describes his father as someone who routinely played jokes on him and belittled him when he was young. Joe felt furious with his father for using his superior position to make him feel even smaller. In a childhood dream, Joe remembers being chased by a giant who fell to his death. In retrospect Joe knows that his dreams were a way of disguising his murderous fury toward his father.

Joe's father embarrassed him in restaurants by making jokes about other patrons who were clearly within earshot. He teased Joe by fooling him with card tricks that he could not figure out. Joe seethed inside over this abuse of size and authority. He played war with toy soldiers. The enemy general was a figure much like Captain Hook in Peter Pan, a swaggering know-it-all, with severe limitations when it came to predicting his impact on others. Joe had the enemy general, a transparent stand-in for his father, die repeated ignominious deaths at the hands of his own soldiers.

As an adult Joe kept finding his father in many other authority figures. He got into no-win battles with them that recreated his childhood trauma. Over the years Joseph learned his own story. He learned to see when he was making a war game out of a seemingly innocuous transaction with a man who for some minor reason reminded him of his father. Now, Joe is excellent at dealing with difficult people. As a negotiator, even with people who actually resemble the childhood picture of his father, Joe is confident. He learned from his story.

My cousin, Sally, grew up with a domineering older sister. Every time Sally made a best friend, she was reinventing the relationship with her domineering older sister. She felt abused, unappreciated, and used. She imagined that her new friend was talking about her behind her back. She twisted what her friend actually said into a disparaging remark. Sally made herself the focus of all criticism voiced by the friend even if it was aimed at someone else. Sally made herself a wreck, but by patient introspection, she learned to release her sister and to recognize when she was projecting these attributes onto other people in her life.

The recent movie *Groundhog Day* depicts this element. The hero of the story is required to repeat the same day over and over until he gets it right. Getting it right means to live the day with kindness and compassion.

Each of us has a story. No matter how attentive our parents tried to be, they still failed us many times. Even if they did their level best, by the nature of the size disparity alone, there were times when we experienced them as capricious and unreliable, if not downright cruel. The way we recognize that we are projecting our story is that we have *urgent feelings that seem to* **scream out for action**. We feel angry, hurt, depressed, ashamed, and poised, to retaliate. We are suspicious. We see ourselves on the receiving end of foul treatment.

By becoming familiar with our childhood story, we can be aware of times when we are reexperiencing it. The more aware we are of our story, the less frequently we let ourselves get caught up in the urgency to act on these emotional remnants of our childhood. We can use *a sense of urgency to act* as a reminder that it is time to be still for a moment and see which memory we are reexperiencing. We can sort out which feelings belong in the present and which come from the past. We can use *a sense of urgency to act* as an opportunity to experience a moment of healing.

When I was little, I made up reasons for my experiences that were based on my littleness and my limited reasoning ability. Those childhood beliefs bias my adult experience right now without my knowing it. Recently, for example, I bought a new modem for my computer and installed it with engineer-like precision. When I turned on my newly installed device, it did not work. I rechecked all connections and reinstalled the software; it still did not work. I became cross, irritated, quietly enraged, and certain that malevolent factors were at work, aimed primarily at me through the sloppy disregard for quality by the computer company. I called them and with prosecutory precision made my case for their lack of quality. Sheepishly, they agreed that I had done everything right and they were remiss in some yet unrecognized way. They agreed to all my terms including the return of their inferior product and all appropriate compensatory measures. I was so focused on being right that I got the modem technical support person to agree that my installation was precise, perfect by any standard. He grudgingly admitted that the fault was clearly with their miserable modem and agreed to its return forthwith. Fooling around with the computer later, I noticed that I had not turned on the modem software. I was reexperiencing a childhood trauma.

As a pre-schooler I talked my mother into buying me a model airplane. When I got home and opened the box there was nothing in it but balsa-wood sticks, tissue paper, glue, and paint. I could not figure out how to assemble the airplane. Despite assurances to the contrary, I was absolutely positive that I had been cheated. I felt betrayed by my mother, certain that she was lying to me, certain that she had made a mistake, certain that she was trying to belittle me. I cried my eyes out over her cruelty and harshness. I remember her utter bewilderment and frustration with me. Years later I learned that balsa, paper, glue, and paint were all a person needs to make a model airplane if he has about ten years more maturation and development.

I relived this experience with my modem with all the urgent feelings of a 4-year-old. As soon as I realized what I had done (or not done) I dashed off an apology to the modem technical support person and faxed it to him. He graciously accepted my apology in a return fax. It took me a while longer to forgive myself, but I learned one important lesson. When I am certain that I am right, I am probably about to relive my model airplane story.

I cannot trust my perceptions. I am biased by my previous experiences. My feelings are automatically triggered more often from past experiences than from current ones. I project the forms of my past experiences onto the world and find the forms over and over again. Therefore, I am never upset for the reason I think!

To be able to use this element of Attitudinal Healing effectively, we need to spend some time mapping the influence of our childhood on the story that we create in our present experience. Each time we experience a strong emotion in adult life that lingers as a distraction, that is, for more than an hour or two, we can be sure that there are contributions from our childhood to this emotion. If we write these in a daily record of upsetting experiences, our Disruptions Notebook (which will be explained in more detail later), we will have the option of looking back over these experiences for recurring themes. These recurring themes make up our stories.

When I make time to be still and listen to the force for guidance on how to return to peace and love, I am usually guided to stay with the feelings and face them as I would turn a ship into the storm. The storm will pass.

4. Forgiveness paves the road to peace.[13]

Am I supposed to forgive everybody? How can I forgive Hitler or Saddam Hussein? Actually, sometimes it may be more difficult to forgive someone for a personal slight. But if I accept forgiveness as a key to peace of mind, I will learn to do it well and some really good things will happen. This does not mean that I will not feel moments of lust or aggression. After all, human beings are animals. Lust is a normal part of the animal procreative cycle and aggression is normal, too, when I fear attack. But I can learn to deal with my lust and fearful, aggressive feelings in my mind rather than in action, so that the amount of time I spend in an unpeaceful state is minimized. It is often more difficult to forgive my own mistakes than to forgive others.

What does it mean to say, "Forgiveness paves the road to peace"? It means that we have the power to begin the process of releasing ourselves from the bonds of our senses and the emotions of blame, guilt and shame. Forgiveness is mostly for ourselves. It rids us of the burden of resentment. When we feel especially wronged, we may not be able to forgive all at once or even by our will alone. Even so, we can start the process. In these situations when we are willing, it is the force that actually accomplishes the forgiving, that is, over a period of time, out of our conscious awareness, our reasoned intuition releases the bonds of resentment.

Emotions are as unreliable as other things sensed by my body. When my son was married, a dear friend did not send him a wedding gift. I was hurt and angry. Later, I learned that my friend had suffered a major trauma prior to the wedding. I recognized what an unreliable guide my hurt feelings were to the reality of life.

If I choose to feel peace, I will. With some practice, it is so. Try this exercise: right now turn your attention to your breathing. Breathe through your nose and from your abdomen. Be aware only of the in and out movement of your abdomen as you breathe. Notice that when you think of your breathing, you are neither thinking of the past nor of the future. You are focused in the here and now, in this moment. Notice also that as you think of your breathing, you are more relaxed. Just by thinking of your breathing, you have chosen peace of mind by minimizing the use of your not-so-reliable senses. During this course you will be asked to make peace of mind your only goal.

I know what you are thinking: "How can peace of mind be my *only* goal? What about education for my children, world peace, feeding the hungry?" Believe it or not, making peace of mind your only goal will not interfere with achieving other things as long as those achievements are comfortable for you. The second time through the lessons we will prove to you that you can achieve what you wish as long as you are at peace with it.

5. Healing is my choice to make.[14]

According to A *Course in Miracles*®, a miracle, a moment of healing, is *a shift in perception that allows us to feel peace of mind*. This shift in perception invariably accompanies an extension of love and compassion to myself or to others when I previously felt anger at myself or someone else. Anger, hurt, guilt, and shame are signs of fear, the absence of love.

When we extend love and compassion from that inner, center part of ourselves to another human being, we are renewing a connection. We are reinforcing a source of affection and inspiration. We are giving our inner essence, with the knowledge that whatever we give, we also receive. We know that our compassion has been received when we can begin to feel warmth coming back.

This process, the extension of love, compassion, miracle, or moment of healing, is the *opposite* of projecting our stories on the world around us. If we can become a good compassion extender, it will help us reduce the time we spend as a projector of our childhood story.

The feeling of shame is a hallmark of reexperiencing our childhood stories. Shame always contains the belief in our smallness and others who are bigger looking down on us. Shame is an intensely felt belief that we have displayed ourselves in a way that will stimulate condemnation in others. This is a potentially debilitating emotional state. Many times in the face of shame we may wish to lash out at others rather than face our own self-condemnation. When we are respectful, we "cool our jets" and recognize that shameful actions do not exist, they are merely errors that need correction. We can correct our errors by gently forgiving ourselves and asking for guidance from the force.

6. Learning is a key to a better life. Teaching is a good way to learn.[15]

When I was in college in New Orleans, I bought the *Times-Picayune* every morning and turned immediately to "Peanuts." One spring day, sitting in Audubon Park, I read a "Peanuts" strip that was so important it changed my life. Lucy, in her psychiatrist's booth, tells Charlie Brown that his problem is that he has no philosophy of life and that he'd better get one right now. Charlie Brown furrows his brow and comes up with: "Life is like an ice cream cone. You have to learn to lick it."

I think Charlie Brown is right on target. *Learning* is the secret to having a satisfying and peaceful life. Circumstances in life always change. Yesterday's answers rarely fit today's problems. All we can be sure of is, with the help of the force, we can solve *any* problem.

Through the years Charlie Brown has been an important teacher to me. So many of his dilemmas are those I face every day, like the annual decision he makes to give Lucy one more chance to hold the football as he kicks it. Every year he kicks at a football that is pulled away at the last instant. Yet he does not become hardened and cynical; instead he gives Lucy one more chance. What an important lesson this is! How only a moment's pride is lost if we give someone one more chance!

The cartoonist Gary Larson has also been an important teacher to me. In one memorable cartoon two vultures sit atop a rotting rhinoceros. One says, "The hot sun, a rotting rhinoceros underfoot, friends flying in from all over . . . you know Fred, it doesn't get any better than this." Can you think of a better lesson in how one's perspective shapes experience? I can't.

When I began to be interested in defense mechanisms, I happened to watch an episode of the old "Batman" television program. I noticed that every comedy sequence illustrated an important defense mechanism. I taught my students defense mechanisms from videotapes of "Batman," and as I taught them, I learned them better myself. I have found that teaching something is a great way to learn it; so, I try to teach what I want to learn. It would be difficult to estimate all that my students have taught me over the years. I know this much; I would not want to practice psychiatry unless I was associated with a teaching program. Teaching and learning from those I teach is invaluable to me.

One thing I am always seeking to learn better is how to tap into the force. In order to do this I must quiet my senses through meditation, learn some elements that can be useful guides, and practice, practice, practice.

7. I have an inner guide, the force, which I can access in quiet moments.[16]

In the quiet I can listen to the force. The force is the intuitive aspect of my unconscious mind that filters through my mature sense of reason—in other words, my reasoned intuition. I may experience an inspired force like the Holy Spirit, God, a Higher Power, or a Life Force. Or I may think of the force as a physiological energy that I may access through reasoned intuition such as my "right brain."

In any case the force is the part of me that I can get in touch with by being still and listening. In this book the force is not capitalized, but if you experience the force as God, the Holy Spirit, a Higher Power, or the Life Force, please capitalize it in your mind.

You are already familiar with this power. I'll bet you have had this experience: you lose your keys and wrack your brain without being able to remember where you left them. Then you decide not to think about the keys for a while and either you remember where you left them or they materialize. That is an example of putting a problem on the back burner to be solved by your inner guide. Another familiar example is that you have a problem you cannot solve. With confidence you say to yourself, "I will sleep on it." The next morning the solution is apparent. These are examples of how you already use the force. If you wish, you can expand your ability to trust the force. It will serve you well.

Being able to trust the force is the most important capacity you can achieve because it will help you in any moment of dilemma. As is written in Ecclesiastes 9:11–12, "The race is not to the swift, nor the battle to the strong, neither yet bread to the wise, nor yet riches to men of intelligence, nor yet favor to men of skill; but time and chance happen to them all. For no one can anticipate the time of disaster." The training that prepares us to deal with our internal sense of disaster is learning to trust our own inner counsel, the force. What do we know about the force?

- The force is a voice of love, compassion, and joining.
- With some practice most people can learn to access the force.
- All people seem to have it.
- It is similar in many people.
- The frightened-self speaks first. To get in touch with the force, we quiet our senses that pick up the noise and static surrounding us and spend some quiet time listening.
- Some people experience the force as thoughts, some as words, some as pictures, and some as a mixture of all of these.

Just use it. Be still and look into yourself. It does not matter if you begin as a skeptic; I certainly did. In fact, it

may be better to begin that way, because to accept something on authority, without data, is not wise. Skepticism
will come and go like every other thought and feeling.

Niels Bohr, one of the fathers of quantum mechan-
ics, visited a physicist friend at his mountain retreat. He
noticed that his friend had a horseshoe nailed above his
cabin door. Dr. Bohr was surprised that he was observing
the old superstition that a horseshoe above the door brings
good luck. He asked, "You don't believe in that, do you?"
His friend answered with a twinkle in his eye, "Of course
not, Niels, but out here they tell me that it works even if
you don't believe in it."

In a similar way, Attitudinal Healing works to increase the quality of life. You do not have to believe in it,
all you have to do is "DO IT."

Some ask, "How can I use it if I do not believe in it?"
It does not matter if you believe in it or not. You do not
have to believe in gravity or electricity for it to work. If it
works, it works! If you meditate daily on these exercises
they will work.

HOW SHOULD I LIVE MY LIFE?

You may be asking, "When are we going to get to the part
about how I should live my life?" We are not going to get
to that part, because the best way to figure out how to live
your life is to look into yourself and trust the force, your
reasoned intuition. Feelings, thoughts, fantasies, and
passions all come and go. You can learn to value a sense
of self, independent of these momentary shifts in the wind
of your mind and emotions. You can begin to experience

yourself as an observer of these emotional weather patterns rather than being ruled by them. *As you learn to value yourself as an observer, you will find Attitudinal Healing.* Attitudinal Healing does not prescribe actions, nor does it specifically prohibit any. Attitudinal Healing is not about actions. It is about observing your feeling, thinking, and sensations. Learning to relax and trust your inner guide, the force, is the most valuable lesson you can learn.

HOW TO USE THE EXERCISES

Here are some guidelines that may be helpful to you. They are only guidelines, and you may choose to modify them to suit whatever works best for you. What works best for me is to read the lesson, meditate, write the lesson on something I look at throughout the day, and, at the end of the day, write in my journal one successful application of the day's lesson or any lesson that led to a change of perception and permitted peace of mind. Sometimes I meditate twice a day, if I had an important feeling that I had insufficient time to experience fully in my morning meditation. Also, I keep a special section of my journal for major disruptions to my peace of mind, a Disruptions Notebook. Keeping detailed notes on disruptions is especially useful. The details should be in two categories: those that describe persons and those that describe my fears about these disruptions. Through detailed descriptions of the persons and fears later in our work, we will reconstruct the important characters and themes of our childhood story.

Read the exercise

The first step is to read the exercise. If you are working with someone, read the exercise together and discuss it for a few minutes. Then meditate.

Meditate

When I meditate, I sit still in an upright chair, in an erect posture with both feet on the floor, close my eyes, and focus on my breathing. Actually, I focus on the rise and fall of my abdomen as I breathe. I breathe through my nose, when that is comfortable for me. I feel the breath come in as my abdomen expands, and I feel the breath flow out as my abdomen contracts. Sometimes I count the out-breaths (1, 2, 3, 4, 5, etc.) and control the pace of my breathing to less than eight breaths per minute. If thoughts drift into my mind, I am aware of them without judging but return to my breath count.

To meditate effectively, I will learn how to handle intrusive thoughts, strong emotions, anger at myself, bodily sensations, the impulse to act, noises, intruders, times when sitting is not relaxing, adding the lesson, how to stop meditation, and how to know I am meditating the right way. Now let us consider how to deal with the normal interruptions to meditation:

Intrusive thoughts

If thoughts or noises come to my mind I give them labels such as "plan," "fantasy," "memory," "sounds." Then I return to an awareness of the rise and fall of my abdomen. I see the words "in" and "out" with the rise and fall of my abdomen. Sometimes it is reasonably easy to follow my breath. At other times the intrusions are relentless. When an intrusion is relentless, I can either accept it or I can try an additional strategy, a mantra, as discussed earlier in this chapter. For the sake of simplicity, take a two-syllable nonsense sound like "trotfoe." Repeat it over and over to yourself in your mind as rapidly as you wish. It will block intrusive thoughts and actually slow down your body's physiology. Alternate calming measures are counting out-breaths and slowing respiration to less than eight breaths per minute.

Strong feelings

If I become disturbed by a feeling, I label it "hate" and try to stay with the feeling, noticing any memories that come to mind until the strong emotion passes. Then I turn my attention back to my breathing, noticing the rise and fall of my abdomen, "in," "out." That is what is meant by following my breath. Because of time limitations there are mornings when I cannot stay with a feeling until it passes. I make a note of that feeling and come back to it in the evening during a special session for meditation.

Anger at myself

It is easy to get annoyed over my inability to stay with my breath. Every time I turn my attention to the rise and fall of my abdomen something else intrudes. The fact of the matter is that no one can stay with his or her breath. It is an exercise that I can get better at but can never master. The key is to be kind and gentle and avoid criticizing myself over not being able to do the impossible. Wouldn't that be a nice lesson to learn!

Bodily sensations

For me, a pain in my body has been a very useful focus. I simply let my mind go as I focus on the pain. In these moments I can recapture painful memories from childhood. I let myself feel strong feelings associated with the childhood memory. When the storm passes, I let the feelings go. For me, painful bodily sensations have been signals of important memories.

Sometimes I cannot get in touch with anything but the bodily pain or the ache. When that happens, I imagine myself breathing warmth into the area of pain and breathing out the ache or pain. Not all bodily sensations are pain. Itches, tingles and others come to mind. Each is focused upon and then, when I am ready, I return to my breath.

The impulse to act

There is no better way to remember something I forgot to do than to begin meditation. I often feel a strong impulse to act, make a telephone call, get a cup of coffee, feed the dogs, fix a door handle. You name it, I will feel an urge to do it during meditation.

One action that tempts me repeatedly is the urge to scratch my nose. What I have learned to do is label this as an "urgency to act." Then if the urge to scratch my nose continues, I slowly and with concentration on the act—

scratch my nose. I stay quiet and pay attention to any feelings and memories associated with this impulse.

Notice this exception to following my breath: *whenever strong feelings or memories associated with strong feelings emerge, I stay with those feelings until they pass.* Then I return to my breath.

Noises

My white miniature poodles, Sam and Sarah, seem to know when I begin meditation because they usually begin chanting (outsiders would label this barking) simultaneously. I notice this, label it "chanting," and return to my breath.

Intruders

We have a rule in our house that anyone can come into the meditation room at any time and meditate. It is open to all, at any time, night or day. Therefore, intruders happen.

The most usual case of intruders led to Two-Dog Meditation. Two-Dog Meditation was born of necessity because Sam and Sarah like to meditate when I do. They actually prefer to meditate in my lap. That is fine. They take turns due to my lap's space limitations. We only have one rule in the meditation room: no chanting. If Sam and Sarah wish to chant they must go to another room in the house, the "barkatorium," a sun room where they may chant to their hearts content. Potential intruders are warned of the peril of treading too close to the house. These intruders may be people, cats, dogs, squirrels, or militant microbes, invisible to the human eye but clearly visible to Sam and Sarah.

Adding the exercise

I say the exercise for the day in my mind over the first few breath cycles and the last few.

When sitting is not relaxing

Sometimes I meditate on an exercise machine or while walking to work. Sometimes I find sitting meditation not relaxing; then I think of the lesson during a repetitive activity such as preparing breakfast or doing the dishes. If you choose to use active time as meditation, the key is to move slowly, be aware of your movements, and perform the movements with ceremony and grace.

Ending the meditation

When my timer goes off at the end of my five to thirty minutes of meditation, I focus on the exercise once more through several breath cycles. Then, slowly and gently, I alert myself, pick up my pencil and get ready to write the exercise.

How I know when I am meditating the right way

Any way I meditate is the right way. There is no perfect meditation, nor is there a wrong meditation. When I spend five-to-thirty minutes sitting, it is right. The only rule is that I be kind to myself during the process.

How I know I am meditating the right length of time

According to Tom Kopka, my meditation teacher, the Dalai Lama says that if the time you choose feels too long, it *is* too long. Reduce the time until it seems to pass quickly.

Write the exercise

Immediately following meditation write the exercise on something, like a card, or piece of paper, so you can make sure to look at it during the day. Each time you look at the exercise, follow your breath, and think of the exercise for a few seconds.

Write in a journal

A few minutes before retiring, turn briefly to the exercise and write down the smallest instance that day when you used it effectively. Try to remember the smallest "healing" of the day, because each journey begins with a single step, and single steps are the building blocks to remember. If you can master the little disruptions, it will then be easier to deal with major conflicts.

> *Example: There is a better way to view the world and I am determined to find it.*[17]

September 4, 1994

Mary acts like a real jerk when she has a big meeting. She ranted and raved around the office today, giving contradictory orders. At first I just saw her as a jerk. Then I thought . . . there is another way to see the world. . . . In that other way all emotions are either love or fear. I realized that she is frightened. I smiled pleasantly and spoke kindly to her. She seemed to calm down.

Sometimes writing about a present application will evoke an episode from the past that conditioned our present response. When that happens, write that one too:

> As I reflect on Mary, that frightened urgent behavior reminds me of Mother when dinner was late. She acted like Father would kill her if he had to wait one second for dinner. I am angry at Mother for being so ineffective.

Here is another example
of an even more difficult shift in perception:
All emotions are either love or fear.[18]

> Molly, my 4-year-old daughter, came into the kitchen whining that her brother, Brad, would not let her watch "Barney" on television. I was on the phone talking to my mother about our vacation. She was insisting on arrangements that were not convenient for our family. I put my hand over the phone and snapped at Molly that she could wait until I got off the phone. I saw her little chin quiver as she turned dejectedly and walked away. In a few moments I recognized that I was being short with Molly because of my irritation with my mother who was being inflexible. I ended the phone call and found Molly scolding her doll for being such a bad girl. I apologized to Molly for being short with her. I explained that I was afraid I was not as good a mother as I wanted to be and had acted angry instead. I do not know if she really understood what I said, but I saw her apologize to her doll.
>
> Looking back I can see how my irritability with Molly was an expression of my own fearfulness that once again I would let my mother dictate vacation

plans in a way that was grossly inconvenient for me, our children, and my husband. Now I realize that my peace of mind is a choice and all feelings are either love or fear. I will put vacation plans on the back burner and ask for guidance from the force.

If, at the end of the day, you cannot think of one time that you applied the exercise then:

1. Write down any exercise that you applied to achieve peace of mind. After a few times through these exercises you will find that your inner guide chooses one that fits the situation so that you will apply an exercise other than the one you are studying. That counts! Write down the application even if it is of a different exercise. If none comes to mind,
2. Write one time that you might have applied the exercise. If none comes to mind,
3. Think of a time in the future that you may be able to use the exercise, and write that. If none comes to mind,
4. Think of a time in the past when you could have used the exercise and write that.

The point of all this is that if you go at this 100 percent, you will write something in your journal at the end of each day, no matter what.

Keep a Disruptions Notebook

If some major disruption to your peace of mind occurs during the day, that is, you are fearful for more than an hour, write about that occurrence in a separate part of your journal, a "Disruptions Notebook." The disruption may have nothing to do with the lesson you are studying. Keep track of it anyway. You will be able to identify the repeating themes that are the most important parts of your childhood story when we synthesize these elements later in the exercises. When writing about a disruption, make a list of the person's qualities or characteristics that you find most frightening. For instance: "Joe was rude, ungrateful, arbitrary, and childish today when he canceled the office picnic. I am afraid that he did that just because he was angry at me after our boss rejected my budget proposal." Those characteristics: "rude, ungrateful, arbitrary, and childish" will be important later in your work. Also write the details of your fears. "I am afraid that the punishment of the whole staff was designed specifically to punish me." That detail will also be important in tracing the themes in your childhood story.

A few concluding thoughts about using the exercises

There are three readings in each exercise: 1, 2, and 3. It is best to go through the exercises three times in sequence, 1 through 56, doing the "1" meditation exercise each day. The second time through do the "2" meditation exercise, and on the third time through, do the "3" meditation exercise rather than the others. In subsequent times through the meditations use whichever one you choose.

It may be useful to vary the amount of effort given to the three parts of daily exercises:

The first time through the exercises

The first time through it might be a good idea to emphasize the thoughts of the exercises by looking at them frequently every day and journaling your successes with the use of them. The first time through you may wish to limit your formal meditation to five to ten minutes at the beginning of the day, because unless you have practiced meditation before, it will be a challenge. After the first time through the exercises, you will be good at it. Remember to use the Disruptions Notebook.

The second time through the exercises

The second time through it might be useful to increase the length of time in formal meditation to ten-fifteen minutes each morning. Continue to look at the exercises throughout the day but be briefer in journaling. Remember the Disruptions Notebook.

The third time through the exercises

The third time through you might increase the time in formal meditation to fifteen-to-twenty minutes each morning and decrease the time in journaling, while keeping the number of times you look at the lesson during the day about the same. Remember the Disruptions Notebook.

You can do the exercises over and over indefinitely. Find the balance of meditation, looking at your lesson card, and journaling that is best for you. The reason for increasing the time in formal meditation is that many people find that meditation is the time when they are most likely to experience peaceful inspiration. If you have that experience, then you will wish to maximize those opportunities. Some people increase the time in formal meditation by doing it twice a day. Some increase meditation time by sitting the first time and the second time in an exercise form. Find the balance that works best for you . . . then do it.

Aesop told about a thirsty crow who found a pitcher with water so low that she could not reach it. The pitcher was too heavy to tip over and too strong to break. Looking inside herself for inspiration she noticed small stones lying about. Picking up these stones and placing them in the pitcher raised the water to a level that she could drink. Inspiration usually provides a way to solve most problems. These solutions usually require brains and heart, not brawn, cunning, and manipulation.

Part II
Meditation
Exercises

WEEK 1

Things Are Not the Way I See Them Now:[19] Perceptions, Preferences, and Their Limitations

During this week you will work on breaking the bonds of certainty in your perceptions and preferences. Certainty keeps you bound to old ways of doing things that have limited value. Certainty makes learning difficult. Certainty keeps you from discovering peace, joy, and happiness. This week will focus on helping you recognize that the way you see the world is limited by your body's sensory organs. You will seek a deeper sense of order by transcending your senses during meditation. The exercises and journaling support meditation.

Similarly, your preferences are distorted. There is nothing wrong with preferences, but insistence on them is a form of attachment that robs you of peace. The first exercises are the hardest ones to implement immediately in your daily life; they will be easier to implement the second time through the exercises. They come first because they are the basis for the rest of the exercises. You need a taste of them even if it is difficult for you to use them effectively at first. Difficulty is a part of life. It is in overcoming difficulty that we gain life's greatest rewards.

Another of Aesop's fables illustrates this point. A farmer gathered his two sons together and told them that he had only two things to leave them: his farmlands and his vineyards. He told them that they could own them together, but they had better not sell them because buried about a foot underground was a secret treasure for them to divide. The sons preferred a relaxed work ethic rather than a strict one. But after the farmer's death, the sons dug up every inch of their farmlands and vineyard. They had turned the soil so vigorously looking for treasure that the land was very well prepared for new growth. That year they had the most bountiful crop ever. Though they found no hidden treasure in the form they expected, they learned a valuable lesson. *There is no treasure without toil.*

For you, too, if you work hard in a relaxed, unhurried way, you will break new ground this week! In addition to reading the exercises, meditating, and journaling each day, remember to write in your Disruptions Notebook any major interruptions to your peace of mind. When you write, be sure to describe the persons you find disruptive in as much detail as possible. Also describe your fears in detail. These details will be important when you use this notebook to map the characters in your story later in the lessons.

EXERCISE 1

THINGS ARE NOT THE WAY
I SEE THEM NOW.[20]

First of all, my perceptions are very limited. My senses of sight, hearing, taste, smell, and touch are able to perceive such a small part of the universe around me that to trust them is pure folly. I am able to perceive only a minuscule portion of events, information, and matter, and what I do perceive is altered by my senses. For example, there is no color without the rods and cones in my eye. People agree, as a group, that since we have similar sensory distortions, we will call certain colors red and others green, but there is no color inherent in what we see. A mosquito, for example, would see colors quite differently.

Second, each perception of mine is influenced by multiple perceptions from the past. Even the pencil in my hand, the chair by the window, my shoes, my hand—whatever I see—is a reflection of my experiences with these things in my past. Much of my past experience with these things is forgotten. But even though they are forgotten, these experiences shape what I see, feel, and think about my environment today. I experience each person in my life in the mold of someone in my past, even though the persons in my past may have little to do with the persons in my present life.

When we were first married, my wife Renée and I entertained infrequently because it seemed such a chore for her. One day, before we were to have some friends over for dinner, I came home to find Renée urgently changing the linens on all the beds. As I pitched in to help, I asked her why we were doing this now. We had not had overnight guests and I could not think of any other reason to be changing the linens. She stated emphatically that she always changed the linens before a dinner party. "Why?" I asked. She thought for a moment and then admitted that she had no idea, but that she was sure that her mother did the same thing.

We called Renée's mother, and after a few flimsy rationalizations Lucille had to admit that she did not know either why she changed the linens, but she was sure that her mother did. Our good luck was that Grandma-Grandma was alive and well, so we called her. She told us that she started changing the linens before having guests for dinner after one evening's gathering when a terrible thunderstorm caused a flash flood. The flood washed away the wooden bridge over the Lynches River which meant that horses could not pull the carriages across to the other side for another day. The dinner guests were forced to stay two nights while the bridge was repaired.

Grandma-Grandma was embarrassed that there were no fresh linens on the beds and she swore that would never happen to her again. So any time friends were invited over in the evening from then on, the linens were changed in advance. She did not want guests to sleep on anything but the freshest linen.

So there we were, changing the linens in Charleston, South Carolina, where the bridges across the Cooper and the Ashley rivers had withstood hurricane after hurricane, where the chances of a repeat of the Lynches River incident were slim to none. There we were, changing the linens for a reason that no longer was pertinent and we were without a clue. I wonder in how many other ways I do things for a reason that no longer exists? This is the kind of mindless, unintended repetition that makes life miserable. More violent examples come to our attention every day in the newspaper or in our daily lives.

Jim was an acquaintance on the school board when my children were midway through their elementary education. He pulled me aside one evening and asked, "Do you have a few minutes?" I said, "Sure." We went to an empty room in the school where he broke down in tears. Sobbing, he told me that he had done something terrible to his son, Dale. He and Dale were putting together some components of Jim's stereo when Dale accidentally pulled a speaker off the table and it smashed to the floor. Jim instinctively lashed out at his son and slapped him across the face. He was horrified that he had done such a violent thing. He asked me if I thought he had harmed Dale irreparably. I told him that I doubted it, but I wondered if anything like that had happened to him when he was a child. He told me a story of a neighborhood girl informing his father that he had called the girl's mother an "old bat." His father immediately accepted the girl's report as true and grabbed him and threw him on a chair to sit there for an hour. He threw him with such force that Jim's breath was knocked out of him and he thought he was going to die. His father ignored his tears and pleading. I told Jim that he might be replaying with his son something like what he had experienced from his father. We talked about how these mindless repetitions are passed down from generation to generation unless we face our feelings toward those who have abused us. Jim went into therapy to face those feelings.

We repeat the past by adopting behavior of a significant person in our childhood. We adopt behavior that we could not question at the time. We adopted it because we feared retaliation, or we wanted to please, or we did not have the cognitive capacity to object effectively when the behavior was adopted.

The linen was changed because the activity was unquestioned. From knowing Renée's grandmother it is easy to understand why she was not questioned. She expected complete obedience from her children, especially her older daughter, Renée's mother. Jim was in no position to defend himself when he was young. He was in no position even to hold onto angry feelings toward his father lest they betray him and increase his father's wrath. In meditation, moments of physical abuse sometimes return as memories when we experience an itch, ache, or pain in some part of our body. Sometimes focusing attention on the area of pain brings back a memory of an old injury. Villains are sometimes associated with that injury. Be sure to write down these memories in your Disruptions Notebook. Later we will explore how to process the angry feelings that arise from those memories.

If I can be still for a moment, I can access the previous experiences that are coloring my perceptions today. Today, give up the sense of limitation that your perceptions hold for you by knowing that you see nothing as it really is now.

At the beginning and end of formal meditation, repeat this lesson to yourself: *Things are not the way I see them now.* Now, when you are ready, begin formal meditation.

First find a comfortable straight back chair. Sit erect in the chair with both feet planted on the floor. Put your hands on your legs or fold them in your lap. Close your eyes and notice your abdomen expand as you say "in" to yourself. Notice your abdomen contract as you say "out." Feel at peace as you follow your breath.

1. This is the first time through the exercises for you. To start out, after your period of formal meditation in the morning, spend time thinking of people in your life with whom you feel an *urgency to act*, just to see what memories come to mind when you think about how you react to these people. These memories play a major role in how you react to the people in your life. Remind yourself of this exercise each time you feel a *sense of urgency* today.

Write on a card or piece of paper that you will look at several times today this exercise: *Things are not the way I see them now*. Look at the exercise several times today and be still for a moment each time you do. When you are still, think about the rise and fall of your abdomen. Follow your breath for just a minute.

Tonight write down one sense of urgency that you dealt with today by reminding yourself that you see nothing as it is now. Write about how that point of view allowed you to shift your perceptual focus to find peace of mind. If you cannot think of one, write one time that you might have used it. If you cannot think of one, write one time that you might use it in the future. If you cannot think of one, do not be discouraged. It will get easier to identify moments of healing as you work your way through the exercises. When you come back to this exercise the second time, you will find it much easier to find such moments in your everyday life.

Here is one example by Bob and Carol Gresk, two teachers of this course: They were driving to a class one night and stopped at a red light before making a left turn when a car behind them began to beep its horn. Bob became frustrated. Carol decided it was a neutral beep. When the left turn was completed, Bob noticed that the car behind was not beeping at them at all but at a car in the right lane beside them. He had developed a fight or flight response on incomplete information. He admitted to himself: *Things are not the way I see them now*.

If a significant disruption to your peace of mind occurs today, write about it in your Disruptions Notebook.

2. You have been through all the exercises at least once. Today, be alert for a *sense of urgency*. Look ahead in the last two minutes of your formal meditation today. Attempt to identify a situation that is likely to stir up a *sense of urgency* in your life today. Imagine stepping back from your urgent feelings, focusing on your breath and feeling peace while dealing with the situation calmly.

At the very end of the meditation see clearly in your mind the picture of your goal, in addition to peace of mind, for this eight weeks. Hold that picture. Notice the details. Feel at peace with that picture.

After meditation, write this exercise on a card or piece of paper that you will look at several times today: *Things are not the way I see them now*. Look at the exercise during the day and be still for a moment each time you do. When you are still, think of the rise and fall of your abdomen as it moves with your breath and feel peace.

If you feel a sense of extreme urgency today that lingers as a distraction for an hour or more, take time to honor those urgent feelings. Then try to link them with the past. When they have passed, make notes in your Disruptions Notebook detailing the characteristics of the people in your disruption as well as your fears. Then relax for a minute or two.

At the end of the day write in your journal one example of using this or any exercise to achieve a shift in perception that brought with it peace of mind. Also, note if that anticipated upsetting instance occurred and, if so, how you handled it. If the situation did not occur, write that down as well.

3. You have been through all the exercises at least twice. Today use your warm, bright light at the end of formal meditation. In the last five minutes of formal meditation remember a past situation that stimulated a storm of urgent feelings. Picture yourself, after the storm has passed, using warm, bright light, first as a ball in your middle that spreads to fill you with warmth. After you experience the warmth and have let it spread to fill your body, then let it spread to those who have acted out a role in your childhood story. *These former tormentors are your teachers.* As always, at the end of the day, write one instance of a moment when you returned to peace of mind by thinking of today's or any exercise.

You are bound to experience resistance to bright light meditation. Here is the way that works: you may notice that there is some difficulty experiencing the building of the warm bright light within you. If that happens stop trying after a few minutes and allow yourself to feel warm feelings. Then proceed with the rest of the exercise. Once you are able to feel the warmth and picture the bright light in subsequent lessons, you may experience your mind wandering as you attempt to share your bright light with another. That means that you are afraid of joining with that other person. Look into yourself to see what you are afraid of. Once you figure that out, you will be able to share your bright light. If the static continues, see what else you may be experiencing toward that other person. Keep working on it, and you will be able to share your bright light.

One additional tip: do not try to share your bright light

until you can feel it warm and spread within yourself. As you focus on experiencing the bright light within yourself, you will actually feel warmer. When a group of people in the same room practice bright light meditation, the room seems to warm up. Once you feel yourself warm up, it is easier to let that warmth spread to someone else. So do not try to spread the warmth until you feel it yourself for at least fifteen seconds.

At the very end of the meditation see clearly in your mind the picture of your goal, in addition to peace of mind, for this eight weeks. Hold that picture. Notice the details. Feel at peace with that picture.

After meditation, write this exercise on a card or piece of paper that you will look at several times today: *Things are not the way I see them now*. Look at the exercise during the day and be still for a moment each time you do. At the end of the day write in your journal one example of using this or any exercise to achieve a shift in perception that brought with it peace of mind. Remember to use your Disruptions Notebook.

Exercise 2

This is an exercise that becomes more and more useful as you learn about your childhood story. So do not be discouraged if it is difficult to apply at first. The basis for this exercise is that all distress comes from multiple sources. When I believe I am angry at someone, that someone stands for many people in my past. When I am afraid of something in the present, it is because it reminds me of something in the past. If I can be still for a while I can find out who this someone in my present life represents from my past. Sometimes this knowledge does not come to mind easily, but if I turn the project over to the force, the memory will return.

Remember that there are no little upsets. The ones that seem little are just the tip of an iceberg. Today, ferret out your upsets, past and present, and put them in the hands of the force for resolution.

Several days ago I was trying to explain something I was working on to my friend, Leo. Leo is usually available to listen but that day he was not, so he cut me off. I was steamed. In my meditation something came to me. I realized that my anger with Leo reminded me of a moment with my father. When I was in college, I attempted to talk to my father about an alternate career path. I think at the time I was considering a career in forestry. My father was working a Sunday *New York Times* crossword puzzle, listening to one baseball game on the radio, and watching another one on television. I said to him, "Dad, what do you think about forestry?" He said, "Mm." I said, "I am thinking of a career in forestry." He said, "Great, medicine is the career of the future." I gave up and watched the base-ball with him. As it turned out, I probably was better suited to medicine than forestry. But I wanted him to be a better listener.

My father was known for his ability to do several things at once, and with all the activity going on that day he was not listening to me. Once I remembered this inci-dent, I turned to my inner guide, "I know that I am blam-ing Leo for something very similar to what I have not yet forgiven my father for, so in regard to my anger with Leo and my father, help me find peace." During the arrival of peace, I also discovered that I was afraid that my idea was not worth much if it did not stimulate rapt attention in others. So my anger contained frightened feelings from the not-too-distant past and fears from adolescence as well.

Stan and I were at a psychiatric meeting in Boston waiting for some friends at Legal Seafood. We had just ordered a beer. Stan took one drink and I saw tears well up in his eyes. I asked, "What's the matter?"

"I hate this beer."

"Do you want something else?"

He sighed and was quiet for a minute or two. "It's not the beer. I am not sure I can talk about what just came to mind." But he did talk about it. The beer reminded him of a smell he had noticed one morning after his parents had been out to a party when he was 13. He had awakened and the whole house smelled of beer. He went in to see his mother and she was in bed with a bandage over her left eye. He was sure that his father had hit her because they had been fighting verbally more and more those days and he imagined that it had finally come to blows. Stan got his .22 rifle and prepared to shoot his father. His mother awakened in time to tell him that it was not as he thought. She had slipped and cut her eye on the night table and his father, a surgeon, had sutured her wound. They had not been fighting; they had just had too much to drink. The beer reminded him of the smell that morning and in an instant he was reminded of the terrible act he had almost committed because he hated his father for causing the family problems at the time.

"When I got mad at this sour-tasting beer, I knew that was not the problem," Stan said.

At the beginning and end of formal meditation repeat this exercise over several breath cycles: *I do not know what distresses me.*

When you are ready, begin formal meditation.

First find a comfortable straight back chair. Sit erect in the chair with both feet planted on the floor. Put your hands on your legs or fold them in your lap. Breathe through your nose when you can. Close your eyes and notice your abdomen expand as you say "in" to yourself. Notice your abdomen contract as you say "out." Feel at peace as you follow your breath.

1. At the end of formal meditation say this exercise to yourself over several breath cycles: *I do not know what distresses me.* Then write this exercise on a card or piece of paper that you will look at several times today: *I do not know what distresses me.* Look at the exercise during the day and be still for a moment each time you do. When you are still, think of your breath and follow it through three breath cycles.

Tonight write down one sense of certainty about what was upsetting you that you dealt with successfully by using this exercise. If you cannot think of one, write one time you might have used it. If you cannot think of one, write one time you might use it in the future. If you cannot think of one, take heart: it will get easier to identify moments of healing as you work your way through the lessons.

2. Anticipate situations in your life today in which you may feel upset. Anticipate using the force to help you find out what is behind that upset. At the very end of the meditation picture clearly in your mind the goal, in addition to peace of mind, for these eight weeks. Hold that picture. Notice the details. Feel at peace with that picture.

After meditation, write this exercise on a card or piece of paper that you will look at several times today: *I do not know what distresses me.* Look at the exercise during the day and be still for a moment each time you do. When you are still follow your breath through three breath cycles.

At the end of the day write in your journal one example of using this or any exercise to achieve a shift in perception that was accompanied by peace of mind. Again, chronicle your success in predicting upsets in life today and how you dealt with other potentially upsetting circumstances. Additionally, write down any past memories that contributed to your current upset.

3. Today use your warm bright light. Remember someone in your past who has contributed to your story. Let yourself feel whatever emotion comes to you. If you feel anger, stay with the feeling until it passes. Then and only then is it time to feel your bright warm light. If the feeling does not pass in one meditation period do not try to use the bright light. When the feelings of anger pass then you can use the bright light.

First, allow yourself to feel the warmth in the middle of your body, around your heart, for a period of time. Then, after you have held the warmth in your middle for a while let it spread to the rest of your body. Then, as you feel the warmth build within you, allow it to spread to those who have participated in your story. Remember, do not try to share your bright light until you can feel it within yourself. As you focus on experiencing the bright light within yourself, you will actually feel warmer. Once you feel yourself warm up, it will be easier to let that warmth spread to someone else.

At the very end of the meditation see clearly in your mind the picture of your goal, in addition to peace of mind, for these eight weeks. Hold that picture. Notice the details. Feel at peace with that picture.

After meditation write down this exercise on a card or piece of paper that you will look at several times today: *I do not know what distresses me.* Look at the exercise during the day and be still for a moment each time you do. At the end of the day write in your journal one example of using this or any exercise to achieve a shift in perception that brought with it peace of mind. Remember your Disruptions Notebook.

I MISPERCEIVE WHAT THINGS ARE FOR.[22]

To see differently, change your preconceptions about what you see. For example, a small table holds my books and pencils right in front of the chair I use for reading and meditating. Even though this table has been around for some time, I do not know its history. I do not know all of what has happened on this table because I have only lived about half the time the table has existed, and even then it has only been mine for about half that time. It could be argued that I know very little about what that table's function has been. And I certainly cannot predict what functions it may serve in the future. Even now I cannot be sure about the many ways this table may serve.

For all I know it may be sharing atoms with me at this moment and I with it. Physicists tell us that while that table looks solid it really is more than 99 percent space. A subatomic particle, like an electron, would pass through it, with the solid aspects of the table appearing to the electron to be miles apart. The table only seems solid because we can discern so little of what there is around us, due to the limitations of our perceptual apparatus. At a subatomic level the table appears very similar to me. It is composed of atoms that are only in small part solid matter and large part energy and information. In fact, the table and I exchange atoms through my breathing in and out, so the table and I are exchanging matter and energy and information. I am not as separate from that table as my senses would have me believe.

Since you experience only about one part in one billion of the total spectrum of energy, information, and matter that exists, do not be certain that what you see is the only or the best view of what actually exists. To help you feel comfortable with uncertainty today, look around and see common objects and admit to yourself that you do not know what they are for.

> I misperceive what this table is for.
> I misperceive what this chair is for.
> I misperceive what this arm is for.
> I misperceive what this nose is for.
> I misperceive what————is for.
> I misperceive what anything is for.

At the beginning and end of formal meditation repeat this exercise over several breath cycles: *I misperceive what things are for.*

When you are ready, begin formal meditation.

First find a comfortable straight back chair. Sit erect in the chair with both feet planted on the floor. Put your hands on your legs or fold them in your lap. Breathe through your nose when you can. Close your eyes and notice your abdomen expand as you say "in" to yourself. Notice your abdomen contract as you say "out." Feel at peace as you follow your breath.

1. After formal meditation write this exercise on a card or piece of paper that you will look at several times today: *I misperceive what things are for.* Look at the exercise during the day and be still for a moment each time you do.

At the end of the day write down one instance that you used comfort with uncertainty to achieve peace of mind. At first this may be a challenge because you may not yet be so sure about your comfort with uncertainty. Take heart. It will be easier the second time around. Here is an example of something that happened today. I was on my way to a meeting at the hospital and got to the parking garage with five minutes to spare. Three people ahead of me had trouble using the automatic card reader that lets us into the garage. I could feel my frightened-self emerging as I became irritable with the bungling that was keeping me waiting. Then I saw what I was doing and I said to myself, "I do not know what this wait is for." I decided that it must be an opportunity for me to calm down. I turned to my breath and relaxed. I decided that I was tense over our operations meeting, but that no matter what happened I was going to be calm. It was a difficult meeting in which we had to decide on budget cutbacks. I look back on that wait as important because it gave me a chance to recognize my tension and to relax. It gave me a chance to reaffirm my decision to be calm in the face of adversity. I was calm and was able to work out reasonable compromises in what might have been a perfectly awful meeting if my frightened-self had been in charge.

2. You have used this exercise at least once before. Today at the end of formal meditation, anticipate a moment in the day when you may be tempted to be certain. You may be able to become more open to your environment if you admit that you do not know what anything is for. Several times throughout the day notice two things around you and admit, "I do not know what this clock is for." "I do not know what this typewriter is for." Then sit still for a minute and follow your breath.

At the very end of the meditation see clearly in your mind the picture of your goal, in addition to peace of mind,

for these eight weeks. Hold that picture. Notice the details. Feel at peace with that picture.

After meditation, write this exercise on a card or piece of paper that you will look at several times today: *I misperceive what things are for.* Look at the exercise during the day and be still for a minute each time you do.

At the end of the day write in your journal one example of effectively using this or any exercise to achieve a shift in perception that permitted peace of mind.

3. You have used this exercise at least twice before. In this application, at the end of formal meditation notice that you do not know what particular things are for. Then let bright light fill you with warmth right in your middle, in your heart. Hold the light there before letting it spread to the rest of your body. When you feel ready, let your warm bright light spill over to bless the things around you. Several times throughout the day admit that you do not know what something is for. Then feel the bright light of warmth within you spill over to the things around you.

At the very end of the meditation see clearly in your mind the picture of your goal, in addition to peace of mind, for these eight weeks. Hold that picture. Notice the details. Feel at peace with that picture.

After meditation write this exercise on a card or piece of paper that you will look at several times today: *I misperceive what things are for.* Look at the exercise during the day and be still for a moment each time you do. At the end of the day write in your journal one example of using this or any exercise to achieve a shift in perception that brought with it peace of mind.

EXERCISE 4

I HAVE GIVEN THINGS ALL THE
SIGNIFICANCE THEY HAVE FOR ME.[23]

Things have no intrinsic value. We use things to prop up sagging self-esteem. We probably do not need props, but at times this is hard to believe. Today, do not indulge in more food, drink, or acquisition of material possessions than you need. Nothing has value separate from your perceptions, so you have given all things the meaning they have for you. Today, think before you act to overvalue things. Think each time you put something into your mouth or pull out your wallet to purchase something. Be still for a moment and just think, "Am I acting automatically or is there something here worth having?"

A good exercise is the three apricot drill. Put three apricots in a cup. Pick up one apricot, look at it, smell it, taste it, eat it. Savor the flavor. Notice that you are thinking of picking up the second apricot before you finish the first. Try to wait until the taste of the first is very slight. Slow down, use all your senses. Do not put the second apricot in your mouth before the taste of the first is almost gone. Today, transfer this thought to all forms of acquisition. Notice an increased awareness of the world as you live in the present. At the beginning and end of formal meditation practice remind yourself that you have given all things the meaning they have for you. Now, when you feel ready, begin formal meditation.

First find a comfortable straight back chair. Sit erect in the chair with both feet planted on the floor. Put your hands on your legs or fold them in your lap. Breathe through your nose when you can. Close your eyes and notice your abdomen expand as you say "in" to yourself. Notice your abdomen contract as you say "out." Feel at peace as you follow your breath.

1. After formal meditation write this exercise on a card or piece of paper that you will look at several times today: *I have given things all the significance that they have for me.* Look at the exercise during the day and be still for a moment each time you do.

Write in your journal one example of using this or any exercise in the day to help you find peace of mind. If you find it difficult to apply this exercise the first time through the book do not be discouraged. Later the usefulness of this exercise will be clearer to you. Remember to use your Disruptions Notebook.

2. This is the second time you have used this exercise. Today spend a few moments looking around. With each object your gaze lights on remind yourself: "I have given this shirt all the meaning it has for me." "I have given this watch all the meaning it has for me." "I have given this chair all the meaning it has for me." After you do this with five things sit quietly and follow your abdomen as it indicates your breath for a few seconds. Then try to think of something you will encounter in your life today that you feel attached to, such as a smile from your supervisor or a ride in the car you enjoy. Say to yourself, "I have given this smile (or car) all the meaning it has for me." At the very end of the meditation see clearly in your mind the picture of your goal, in addition to peace of mind, for these eight weeks. Hold that picture. Notice the details. Feel at peace with that picture.

After meditation write this exercise on a card or piece of paper that you will look at several times today: *I have given things all the significance that they have for me.* Look at the exercise during the day and be still for a moment each time you do.

At the end of the day write in your journal one example of using this or any exercise to achieve a shift in perception that brought with it peace of mind.

3. This is the third time you applied this exercise. At the end of formal meditation begin just as you did the second time: "I have given this typewriter all the meaning it has for me." "I have given this clock all the meaning it has for me." Then add bright light to warm your heart, your body, and then the things you notice.

Remember some attachment in the past. If that attachment causes some significant disruption in feelings, write about it in your Disruptions Notebook for later study. Feel all the feelings associated with that attachment. When the feelings pass, let the attachment go and let the warm bright light fill your heart, and then your body. When you are ready, let it spread to the person or thing in your past attachment.

At the very end of the meditation see clearly in your mind the picture of your goal, in addition to peace of mind, for these eight weeks. Hold that picture. Notice the details. Feel at peace with that picture.

After meditation, write this exercise on a card or piece of paper that you will look at several times today: *I have given things all the significance that they have for me.* Look at the exercise during the day and be still for a moment each time you do.

At the end of the day write in your journal one example of using this or any exercise to achieve a shift in perception that brought with it peace of mind.

Exercise 5

I VIEW A FICTIONAL WORLD.[24]

In the book *Love Is The Answer,* by Gerald Jampolsky, M.D., and Diane Cirincione, a cartoon depicts a man with a projector in his head throwing images from his mind onto the screen of the world around him.[25] In the dramatic moments of life our perceptions of the characters in the story we see are heavily colored by our past experiences. We become the screenwriter, director, and star of our own independent productions. In childhood we made up a story to explain our feelings. We project the outlines of that story on our adult experience.

We each have a unique set of emotional characteristics that we attribute to other people. These emotional characteristics come from the way we experienced important beings through our child's mind and child's eyes. We tend to reinvent the beings in our childhood drama over and over again in our adult lives. *We reinvent past troubling relationships until we learn to forgive the villains in them.* One way to think of this is that our stories are the doors to discovering the lessons we have yet to learn.

When I was a very little boy, I remember going outside with my mother to enjoy a sunny day. The next thing I remember is being alone in our yard with a herd of cattle. I could see my mother on the porch, but I could not get to her because of all the cattle in the way. I was terrified. I felt lost, abandoned, doomed by the crushing herd around me. I felt smothered even though there was plenty of air. I was terrified that all was lost.

Today, when I first encounter a problem, I am likely to believe that it is too big and too difficult for me to handle.

I feel that my breath is about to be cut off and I will smother in my own fears of doom. It is as if I were 3 years old again and separated from my mother by a wall of gigantic cattle. Then I remind myself of the second part of the story. I do not remember this, but my mother tells me that she was distraught when the cattle from a neighbor's farm came into the yard. She could not see me and I was making no sounds. But then as she began to despair, I came pushing my way through the cows. They moved aside as I shoved them, to make my way to the porch and my mother.

Today, I remind myself that if I could shove my way through cows when I was 3, chances are that I will find a solution to today's problem. But my first impulse is to view problems as insurmountable and the people around me as immovable obstructions who cut off my life's breath. A sunny day may make me feel tired at first as if the cows might soon appear. Sometimes I feel suspicious when people invite me to an outdoor activity, as if they were trying to lull me into a trap.

Find times when you tend to predict worse outcomes for yourself than usually happen and link it to a time in your childhood when you tried to do something you could not, or could do only with great difficulty. Use this exploration of your story to help overcome an obstacle of unwarranted pessimism.

Do not be discouraged if you have trouble doing this the first time through the exercises. Not every exercise will immediately yield results the first time you use it. At the beginning and end of formal meditation, repeat this exercise over several breath cycles: *I view a fictional world.*

Now, if you feel ready, begin formal meditation.

First find a comfortable straight back chair. Sit erect in the chair with both feet planted on the floor. Put your hands on your legs or fold them in your lap. Breathe through your nose when you can. Close your eyes and notice your abdomen expand as you say "in" to yourself. Notice your abdomen contract as you say "out." Feel at peace as you follow your breath.

1. At the end of meditation write this exercise on a card or piece of paper that you will look at several times today: *I view a fictional world.* Look at the exercise during the day and be still for a moment each time you do. At the end of the day write in your journal a successful application of this exercise. Do not be hard on yourself if this exercise is difficult to apply at first. Just give it your best effort. Remember to use your Disruptions Notebook.

2. In the last two minutes of your formal meditation think about someone you are likely to meet today. Make it a point to treat this person with reverence and respect in your imagination. Try to learn one lesson from someone you meet today and write that lesson in your book tonight.

At the very end of the meditation see clearly in your mind the picture of your goal, in addition to peace of mind, for these eight weeks. Hold that picture. Notice the details. Feel at peace with that picture.

After meditation write this exercise on a card or piece of paper that you will look at several times today: *I view a fictional world.* Look at the exercise during the day and be still for a moment each time you do. At the end of the day write in your journal one example of using this or any exercise to achieve a shift in perception that brought with it peace of mind.

3. Today, learn a lesson from someone, someone in the past who gave you a hard time. Let yourself feel the full brunt of your angry feelings toward that person. When the storm of feelings has passed, let your warm bright light build in your heart. Hold it there. Let the warm bright light spread over your body. When you are ready, let it spread to the people in your past you wish to heal.

At the very end of the meditation see clearly in your mind the picture of your goal, in addition to peace of mind, for these eight weeks. Hold that picture. Notice the details. Feel at peace with that picture. After meditation write this exercise on a card or piece of paper that you will look at several times today: *I view a fictional world.* Look at the lesson during the day and be still for a moment each time you do.

At the end of the day write in your journal one example of using this or any exercise to achieve a shift in perception that brought with it peace of mind. Remember to use your Disruptions Notebook.

EXERCISE 6

I CANNOT SEE WHAT IS BEST FOR ME.[26]

It is difficult to know my own best interests when I know that I react to the world as if it were full of monstrous, immovable cows. In addition, my senses, independent of my childhood story, give me a very limited view of the known world. It is very hard for me to know my own best interests, when I perceive so little of what exists. When I ask for guidance, it is best that I ask for the freedom to trust the force. Knowing that I cannot foresee all contingencies is a powerful position, because it releases me from the illusion of certainty. The only thing I need be certain about is that no matter what the situation, I can access the power within me for help and guidance. This helpful voice is a quiet voice that can be experienced in stillness.

In my practice periods today I will think of the events I would wish to influence and say:

In the case of———, I would like———to happen.

Then I will recognize that I do not know and cannot possibly perceive if what I wish for would be best by saying:

But since I cannot see what is best for me, I will trust the force.

At the beginning and end of formal meditation repeat this exercise over several breath cycles: *I cannot see what is best for me.*

Now, when you feel ready, begin formal meditation.

First find a comfortable straight back chair. Sit erect in the chair with both feet planted on the floor. Put your hands on your legs or fold them in your lap. Breathe through your nose when you can. Close your eyes and notice your abdomen expand as you say "in" to yourself.

Notice your abdomen contract as you say "out." Feel at peace as you follow your breath.

1. After meditation write this exercise on something you will look at throughout the day: *I cannot see what is best for me.*

Write in your journal an example of using the exercise at the end of the day. Remember to use your Disruptions Notebook.

2. In this application try one addition to the first practice. Recognize a grievance toward someone in your environment and write that grievance in your Disruptions Notebook. Then let yourself feel the full extent of your angry feelings toward that person. Do not be afraid to feel strong angry emotions and vivid fantasies involving that person. When the storm has passed, turn your grievances over to the force.

"As for X, I hate his guts, I would like to strangle him slowly and watch him flail in vain as his purple tongue protrudes from his blue lips, while he gasps unsuccessfully to hold onto the last vestige of his miserable life. As his life drains out of him, I would like to throw his limp, lifeless body into a deep watery grave." And then the storm passes. *"But, because I know that I cannot know what would be best, I ask for help in releasing my anger to trust the force.*

At the very end of the meditation see clearly in your mind the picture of your goal, in addition to peace of mind, for these eight weeks. Hold that picture. Notice the details. Feel at peace with that picture.

After meditation, write this exercise on a card or piece of paper that you will look at several times today: *I cannot see what is best for me.* Look at the exercise during the day and be still for a moment each time you do. At the end of the day write in your journal one example of using this or any exercise to achieve a shift in perception that brought with it peace of mind.

3. The third variation adds warm, bright light meditation to the process. If you are good at this now, you can be sure that as you practice it each day you will get better as you engage your disruptors with the warm bright light that radiates from you. Attempt to do this only after you have honored and experienced your angry feelings. Be thankful for your angry feelings because they are your beacons for healing. After angry feelings pass let the warm bright light fill your heart. Hold it there. Let it spread to the rest of your body. When you feel ready, let it spread to those you wish to heal. As you heal them and release them from all blame, you heal yourself.

At the very end of the meditation see clearly in your mind the picture of your goal, in addition to peace of mind, for these eight weeks. Hold that picture. Notice the details. Feel at peace with that picture. After meditation, write this exercise on a card or piece of paper that you will look at several times today: *I cannot see what is best for me*. Look at the exercise during the day and be still for a moment each time you do. At the end of the day write in your journal one example of using this or any exercise to achieve a shift in perception that brought with it peace of mind. Remember your Disruptions Notebook.

EXERCISE 7

THERE IS A MORE PEACEFUL WAY TO SEE THE WORLD.[27]

Today, as problems arise, look inside yourself and find that you can access your inner guide to help overcome fear. Be still for a moment and then go home. Home is not a house. It is not a place at all. It is a sense of peace within yourself. Turn problems over to the force. Know that eventually a solution will bubble up from within you, or a seeming chance meeting will shed light on what earlier seemed impossible. In order to see the world differently, quiet the static of your senses and access a deeper truth through meditation.

Try to be especially attuned to the grievances you feel. Grievances are a form of fear. Do not forget that both big and small grievances disrupt your inner peace. Try to identify grievances as you become aware of them and turn them over to your inner guide to help you process these distractions. You can view the world with peace of mind, if you are determined to do so. Here are the steps:

1. Recognize the grievances that disrupt your peace of mind.
2. Recognize that grievances are a form of fear. Try to identify your fear. Sit with your storm of feelings until they pass.
3. Acknowledge a desire to accomplish a change of mind to reestablish peacefulness.
4. Ask the force to guide you to peace of mind.

At the beginning and end of formal meditation repeat this exercise over several breath cycles: *There is a more peaceful way to see the world.*

Now, when you are ready, begin formal meditation.

First find a comfortable straight back chair. Sit erect in the chair with both feet planted on the floor. Put your hands on your legs or fold them in your lap. Breathe through your nose when you can. Close your eyes and notice your abdomen expand as you say "in" to yourself. Notice your abdomen contract as you say "out." Feel at peace as you follow your breath.

1. After meditation write this exercise on a card or piece of paper that you will look at several times today: *There is a more peaceful way to see the world.* Look at the exercise during the day and be still for a moment each time you do.

Write in your journal an example of using this or any exercise today. Do not forget to use your Disruptions Notebook.

2. In the last few minutes of your formal meditation today anticipate a situation in which you are likely to feel your peace of mind disrupted. Practice sitting still with those disrupted feelings, using the four steps above to refocus. Then focus on your breath and watch the disruption pass. Be sure to write about what disruptions you anticipated before the beginning of the day and how your anticipation worked out at the end of the day. This gives you an opportunity to test your accuracy at anticipating disruptions.

At the very end of the meditation see clearly in your

mind the picture of your goal, in addition to peace of mind, for these eight weeks. Hold that picture. Notice the details. Feel at peace with that picture. After meditation write this exercise on a card or piece of paper that you will look at several times today: *There is a more peaceful way to see the world.* Look at the exercise during the day and be still for a moment each time you do.

At the end of the day write one example in your journal of using this or any exercise to achieve a shift in perception that brought with it peace of mind. Remember your Disruptions Notebook.

3. Today, in the last few minutes of your formal meditation remember a disruption to your peace of mind from the past. Sit still for a moment and picture the persons involved in that disruption. Honor your strong feelings and write this example of disruption in your Disruptions Notebook. When the storm of feelings passes, feel a warm bright light fill your heart. When you are ready, let that warm, bright light spread all over your body. Then imagine each of the offenders filled by your bright light as you feel your tension with them fade away. Today, use this bright light meditation when you feel someone or something disrupt your peace of mind. At the very end of the meditation see clearly in your mind the picture of your goal, in addition to peace of mind, for these eight weeks. Hold that picture. Notice the details. Feel at peace with that picture.

After meditation write this exercise on a card or piece of paper that you will look at several times today: *There is a more peaceful way to see the world.* Look at the exercise during the day and be still for a moment each time you do.

At the end of the day write in your journal one example of using this or any exercise to achieve a shift in perception that brought with it peace of mind. Remember your Disruptions Notebook.

WEEK 2

Emotions May Be Viewed as either Love or Fear.[28]

There is only one driving psychological force, LOVE. Aggression (hate, anger, envy, jealousy, guilt, shame) is a condition of fear. Fear arises when we think that we cannot gratify our loving wishes. Fear is a secondary condition. Either I feel love or fear. When I act irritably, I am frightened and calling out for help and compassion. When I extend compassion to an angry person, I am choosing joining over separation.

In addition to reading the exercises, meditating and journaling each day, remember to write in your Disruptions Notebook any major interruptions to your peace of mind this week. When you write in your Disruptions Notebook, be sure to describe the persons you find disruptive in as much detail as possible. This detail will be important when you use the notebook to map the characters in your story later in the lessons. Also write the details of your fears in as much detail as you can in order to help you reconstruct your childhood story.

EXERCISE 1

EMOTIONS MAY BE VIEWED
AS EITHER LOVE OR FEAR.[29]

I have two sets of feelings. One set comes from my frightened-self. The other set comes from my loving-self. When I am experiencing feelings from my frightened-self and am stuck in them, I experience hell on earth. One aspect of this hellish experience is that I believe I need someone else to behave in a certain way in order to redeem me, to return me to a feeling of safety. This living hell includes a belief that there is only one way to experience peace and that way requires a specific action on the part of someone else.

For years I considered myself the expert in my family on holiday lighting. My job, as I saw it, was to arrange a tasteful array of lighting for our outdoor Christmas decorations. One year, Renée, my wife, objected to the outdoor lighting as being too bright. I was incensed. How could anyone question The Emir of Illumination? That was like telling Mozart his symphony had too many notes.

I had tastefully arranged 2,000 watts of halogen floodlights to illuminate our traditional display of holiday fruits, wreaths, and garlands. Moreover, I arranged for them to come on at dusk and turn off four hours later. What a breakthrough in technology! Why was I not receiving the accolades that would naturally accompany such a miracle of electronic ingenuity? Not only was I not receiving the adulation that my frightened-self knew, beyond a shadow of a doubt, that I deserved, but instead Renée seemed disdainful. Undeterred, each day when I left for work I made sure the lighting was just as I desired. And each day when I returned home, half of my masterwork had been unplugged. When, with certainty of purpose I re-plugged it, Renée commented, "It looks like a used car lot." My 1200-pound frightened-self burst out like the Incredible Hulk. I shouted that she knew nothing about lighting and that I was the acknowledged expert in the field. She replied that the neighbors were afraid that aircraft might land here in the fog because we lit up the whole street. I became even more enraged. The neighbors could just move if they didn't like it; they were not going to interfere with my artistry. It was the first amendment that was at stake here, maybe even the freedom of the entire planet. I stomped into the backyard where I noted that I could easily read my watch despite the fact there was no light in the backyard, not even a moon. All that light was coming from my "tasteful 2000 watts" in the front yard. I looked on my masterpiece with a fresh eye. It *was* too bright! Why was I being so bull-headed?

During meditation the next morning I remembered a time in my adolescence when my mother was critically ill. I could not help her, so I busied myself with the holiday lighting and was thanked by my family for recapturing the holiday spirit. It was all I could do then to deal with my sense of injustice in the world. I did not know who would look after my interests if my mother died; I was sure that I could not take care of myself.

But now no one was sick. I had come to terms with my need for someone to look after me. There were other ways I could contribute to the holiday. Why was I acting as if all I could do was the lighting? I had not integrated that painful memory from the past into my adult experience. Once I did, I calmed down and was able to laugh at myself. I rearranged a less bright light source and reestablished my claim to the lighting hall of fame. The holidays were fine.

While I was in my frightened-self, I believed the only way I could feel peace was if my wife accepted my way of doing things. This is what is referred to as a *special relationship*. What is special about it is that we are sure, absolutely positive, that the only solution is for the other person in that relationship to behave exactly as we wish. A special relationship is the opposite of a mature relationship. A mature relationship is not based on getting someone else to do exactly as we wish. A mature relationship is based on loving kindness and the desire that the other person experience her freedom and develop her talents. Special relationships are based on the fear that we cannot have our loving wishes fulfilled. When I was a child and my mother was ill, I was afraid. That fear was normal; now it is not. With that understanding I can choose to forego my special relationship and return to a more mature one.

My friend, Jim, found a note at work from his immediate supervisor, Herb, that excoriated Jim's recent proposal on automation of their plant. Jim knew this harshness was unlike his friend and colleague and went to see him. Herb was stone faced. Jim mentioned that he had read the memo about his proposal. Herb looked at his desk and grunted. This was not at all like Herb. Jim asked, "Herb, is there something wrong?" Tears welled up in Herb's eyes. His wife Anne had recently found a lump in her breast and he was terrified about the biopsy today. They had four small children and he was afraid they might not have a mother for long. He had lost his own mother when he was 9 and life had not been the same after that. Jim comforted Herb and put his proposal on the back burner. Later, Herb's wife's biopsy brought good news. By extending himself in love rather than anger Jim did more good than he would have with ten great proposals.

At the beginning and end of formal meditation repeat this exercise over several breath cycles: *Emotions may be viewed as either love or fear.*

Now, when you feel ready, begin formal meditation.

First find a comfortable straight back chair. Sit erect in the chair with both feet planted on the floor. Put your hands on your legs or fold them in your lap. Breathe through your nose when you can. Close your eyes and notice your abdomen expand as you say "in" to yourself. Notice your abdomen contract as you say "out." Feel at peace as you follow your breath.

1. After meditation write this exercise on a card or piece of paper that you will look at several times today: *Emotions may be viewed as either love or fear.* Look at the exercise during the day and be still for a moment each time you do.

At the end of the day write in your journal one example of using this or any exercise to achieve a shift in perception that brought with it peace of mind.

2. In the last few minutes of formal meditation think of someone whom you want to behave in a certain way today. Predict how that person will behave and imagine how you might react to that experience. This evening check out your prediction and write down one moment that you were able to see someone who was certain, cranky, or harsh as frightened and calling out for help.

At the very end of the meditation see clearly in your mind the picture of your goal, in addition to peace of mind, for these eight weeks. Hold that picture. Notice the details. Feel at peace with that picture.

After meditation write this exercise on a card or piece of paper that you will look at several times today: *Emo-*

tions may be viewed as either love or fear. Look at the exercise during the day and be still for a moment each time you do. At the end of the day write in your journal one example of using this or any exercise to achieve a shift in perception that brought with it peace of mind.

3. In the last few minutes of formal meditation remember that one of the illusions you experience when you are in your frightened-self is that each person is separate rather than being joined as a part of the life force. Remember today in your meditation that you are connected with everything around you and exchanging atoms with everything in your environment. Remember someone who stimulated a fearful response in you in the past. Let yourself feel the strong feelings associated with that memory. When the feelings have quieted, implement bright light meditation seeing yourself as connected to that person you tend to see as separate from you through your warm bright light.

At the very end of the meditation see clearly in your mind the picture of your goal, in addition to peace of mind, for these eight weeks. Hold that picture. Notice the details. Feel at peace with that picture.

After meditation, write this exercise on a card or piece of paper that you will look at several times today: *Emotions may be viewed as either love or fear.* Look at the exercise during the day and be still for a moment each time you do. At the end of the day write in your journal one example of using this or any exercise to achieve a shift in perception that brought with it peace of mind.

MY STRESSORS ARE ANGRY FEELINGS
IN MY MIND.[30]

Our automatic response to the world is to identify things that stress us as being outside ourselves. That is an illusion. Our responses to the world are preprogrammed by experiences in our past, many of which are forgotten. That does not mean that an irritable colleague or disappointment in a loved one is inconsequential, but it does mean that the spin we put on these experiences comes from childhood when we were less capable than now to see alternatives. That helpless and often hopeless spin is often more important than the external realities themselves.

When I was a young boy, I spent a night with my cousin, Dan. His father came home from the office in a sour mood and yelled at his son, "Dan, get your bicycle out of the middle of the driveway!" Dan scurried toward the door. On the way he ran across a crayon that belonged to his little sister Mary. Dan shouted, "Mary, get your crayons out of the middle of the floor." Mary jumped to attention and ran to pick up her crayons. On the way she passed a potted palm in the hallway. She paused for a moment, turned toward the palm and shouted, "Shut up, tree!"

Obviously, it was not the bicycle, crayon, or tree that were the problems. My uncle brought a grievance home from work, and the stressor spread like wildfire. Similarly, by choosing peace rather than blame, you can decrease stress in a ripple effect.

In his younger adult life my cousin Dan reacted to disorder as something catastrophic. He withdrew passively into a world of inaction rather than face the mess of day-to-day living. He could not avoid his internal critic. Passivity seemed to be the only answer. He experienced this dilemma: "If I cannot avoid my screaming father, why try?" Later, in therapy, he began to be able to feel aggression toward his father and to express it in his imagination. Later still, he was able to forgive his father who was clearly reenacting what his own father had done to him. The stories of Dan's father's abuse by his own father were legendary in the community. With this insight Dan began to see his own passivity as a choice he made to avoid the ghost of his father, his inner critic. Once Dan experienced a choice, he chose to deal with this inner critic in his imagination. With some practice he experienced a return of energy and initiative.

At the beginning and end of formal meditation repeat this lesson over several breath cycles: *My stressors are angry feelings in my mind.*

Now, when you are ready, begin formal meditation.

First find a comfortable straight back chair. Sit erect in the chair with both feet planted on the floor. Put your hands on your legs or fold them in your lap. Breathe through your nose when you can. Close your eyes and notice your abdomen expand as you say "in" to yourself. Notice your abdomen contract as you say "out." Feel at peace as you follow your breath.

1. After meditation write this exercise on a card or piece of paper that you will look at several times today: *My stressors are angry feelings in my mind.* Look at the exercise during the day and be still for a moment each time you do.

At the end of the day write in your journal one example of using this or any exercise to achieve a shift in per-

ception that brought with it peace of mind. Remember your Disruptions Notebook.

2. In the last few minutes of formal meditation focus on one particular person you are likely to meet today toward whom you are likely to develop a grievance. When you meet that person today, keep peace of mind as your only goal. In meditation this morning imagine doing that in your mind. Remember when you do encounter that person, your ego will speak first. Listen to your frightened-self, then go deeper and listen to the force, letting peace, rather than your grievances, fill you.

At the very end of the meditation see clearly in your mind the picture of your goal, in addition to peace of mind, for these eight weeks. Hold that picture. Notice the details. Feel at peace with that picture.

After meditation write this exercise on a card or piece of paper that you will look at several times today: *My stressors are angry feelings in my mind.* Look at the exercise during the day and be still for a moment each time you do. When you are still, follow your breath, "in" and "out" as your abdomen rises and falls with your breath. Follow your breath through several cycles. Be at peace.

At the end of the day write in your journal one example of using this or any exercise to achieve a shift in perception that brought with it peace of mind. Remember your Disruptions Notebook.

3. In the last minutes of formal meditation today remember someone in the past for whom you feel a strong grievance. Let yourself feel the full force of blame toward that person until the storm of feeling passes. When it does, let a warm bright light fill you. First feel a warm bright light in the middle of your body, in your heart. Then when the warmth fills your heart let it expand to all your body. When you are thoroughly warmed by the light, let it flow from you to an image of the other person and envelop them in the warm bright light of kindness and compassion.

At the very end of the meditation see clearly in your mind the picture of your goal, in addition to peace of mind, for these eight weeks. Hold that picture. Notice the details. Feel at peace with that picture.

After meditation write this exercise on a card or piece of paper that you will look at several times today: *My stressors are angry feelings in my mind.* Look at the exercise during the day and be still for a moment each time you do. When you are still, follow your breath, "in" and "out" as your abdomen rises and falls with your breath. Follow your breath through several cycles. Be at peace.

At the end of the day write in your journal one example of using this or any exercise to achieve a shift in perception that brought with it peace of mind. If you find your compassion disrupted today for a significant length of time by any occurrence, be sure to note that in your Disruptions Notebook.

EXERCISE 3

PERCEPTIONS ARE EITHER FOR SEPARATION OR FOR JOINING.[31]

I can either see myself as similar or dissimilar to any person in the world. Today I will see similarities rather than differences. I will be a "love-finder" rather than a "fault-finder."[32]

When I was in fifth and sixth grade, there was another boy my age who went to the same school whose nickname was "Big Bubba." When I was in sixth grade, Bubba was about six feet tall and heavy as a horse. Not only was he big, but he was ugly, as ugly as a bull dog that looks like its face was pushed in by a snow plow. He had curly black hair and a gap between his two front teeth. It was said that he once got angry at a neighbor, lifted his car and turned it over just out of meanness. I was scared to death of Bubba, but instead of admitting my fear, I fought him almost every day. Bubba may have been strong as an ox, but he was slow. Otherwise he would have crushed me like an ant. He called me "Yankee" because a branch of my family lived in the North. In South Carolina, in the early 1950s, being called a "Yankee" was an invitation for a fight. So Bubba and I fought just about every chance we got. It actually wasn't much of a fight. He teased me; I took a swing at him which usually grazed his arm or shoulder. He grinned and I ran like a rabbit. It made school much more stressful than it had to be. Tension mounts when you know that each day you have to fight a giant. I was glad when we moved to another school where we were in different classes. It is very painful to be afraid and ready to attack every day. It never occurred to me that I had a choice in my response to Bubba.

When I went back for my high school reunion fifteen years after graduation, my wife and I were seated at the same table as Bubba, now called Robert, and his wife. Robert was the same; he still had a gap between his front teeth, but his ugliness was now in fashion. It was called Charles Bronson good looks. He had gone to law school and become a successful attorney in the town where I grew up. That evening I really got to know Robert for the first time. We shared what we had done since high school. Robert had gone to the University of South Carolina and continued on for law school. He met his wife in law school. She was a small, quiet person with a quick sense of humor. I thought he and his wife were great and so did Renée. Looking back on it, the only thing that changed was my attitude. Robert was pretty much the same. He argued the same way he did when we were in grade school. He still blamed the damn Yankee carpetbaggers for many of the local problems. I had changed though. I found similarities not differences and most important—I did not hit him! It made the evening a pleasant one, and it taught me a lesson.

At the beginning and end of formal meditation repeat this exercise over several breath cycles: *Perceptions are either for separation or for joining.*

Now, when you are ready, begin formal meditation.

First find a comfortable straight back chair. Sit erect in the chair with both feet planted on the floor. Put your hands on your legs or fold them in your lap. Breathe through your nose when you can. Close your eyes and notice your abdomen expand as you say "in" to yourself.

Notice your abdomen contract as you say "out." Feel at peace as you follow your breath.

1. After meditation write this exercise on a card or piece of paper that you will look at several times today: *Perceptions are either for separation or for joining.* Look at the exercise during the day and be still for a moment each time you do. When you are still, follow your breath, "in" and "out" as your abdomen rises and falls with your breath. Follow your breath through several cycles. Be at peace.

At the end of the day write in your journal one example of using this or any exercise to achieve a shift in perception that brought with it peace of mind. Remember your Disruptions Notebook.

2. Think ahead to the person you will encounter today with whom you may have difficulty seeing similarities. In the last few minutes of your formal meditation anticipate this encounter and anticipate dealing with it effectively.

At the very end of the meditation see clearly in your mind the picture of your goal, in addition to peace of mind, for these eight weeks. Hold that picture. Notice the details. Feel at peace with that picture.

After meditation, write this exercise on a card or piece of paper that you will look at several times today: *Perceptions are either for separation or for joining.* Look at the exercise during the day and be still for a moment each time you do. When you are still, follow your breath, "in" and "out" as your abdomen rises and falls with your breath. Follow your breath through several cycles. Be at peace.

At the end of the day write in your journal one example of using this or any exercise to achieve a shift in per-

ception that brought with it peace of mind. Remember your Disruptions Notebook.

3. Today, remember someone from your past from whom you've felt a severe separation. Let yourself feel the full force of any aggressive emotion toward that person. Then, when the storm of aggressive feelings passes, let the warm bright light build in you. First feel a warm bright light in the middle of your body and in your heart. Then when the warmth fills your heart, let it expand to all your body. When you are thoroughly warmed by the light, let it flow from you to an image of the other person and envelop him in the warm bright light of kindness and compassion.

At the very end of the meditation see clearly in your mind the picture of your goal, in addition to peace of mind, for these eight weeks. Hold that picture. Notice the details. Feel at peace with that picture.

After meditation, write this exercise on a card or piece of paper that you will look at several times today: *Perceptions are either for separation or for joining.* Look at the exercise during the day and be still for a moment each time you do. When you are still, follow your breath, "in" and "out" as your abdomen rises and falls with your breath. Follow your breath through several cycles. Be at peace.

At the end of the day write in your journal one example of using this or any exercise to achieve a shift in perception that brought with it peace of mind. Remember your Disruptions Notebook.

MY ANGRY THOUGHTS AND FEELINGS PREVENT ME FROM SEEING A MEANINGFUL WORLD.[33]

If I do not learn to recognize and process my angry feelings I may suppress those feelings and end up feeling alienated from the people around me. It is in my best interest to recognize and process my angry feelings. Here is one way to process angry feelings:

Today, I will use as a guide the Bible, Luke 17:3. "If your brother offends you, rebuke him and if he repents, forgive him." Here is a way to use this verse. I will not suppress my angry feelings. This is the single most important thing I can do because it is the key to forgiveness. How can I forgive someone that I never felt free to blame? I will think of blame as a stepping-stone to forgiveness. If a person irritates or angers me today, I will rebuke that person in my imagination, then imagine her apologizing, and finally imagine myself forgiving her. I can write this dialogue rather than just imagining it if it helps me. Some people I know do this better with pictures in their mind than with writing letters. One friend imagines mowing down people who irritate him with a sub-machine gun. That is acceptable, too. In my work book I can write an imagined dialogue. With practice I can do this in my mind, in seconds.

Once I can do that, I am handling hate happily. The advantages to handling hate happily are several:

- With some practice it take less time than stewing.
- The energy that I once used to hate and the energy I might have used to suppress the hate can now be

used for other things like *careful observation of others* to see what frightens them. If I imagine the apology carefully (from the other person's point of view) I will come up with some good hypotheses about what motivates him. This may also be a hint about what stimulates me to split off that part of myself that I project onto that other person. Then I can use my aggressive energy for initiative in other endeavors.

- And, I find that forgiveness is even sweeter if I can welcome aggressive emotions without feeling compelled to act on them. This exercise can be done within myself, where aggression ultimately must be worked out. No mean action or nasty verbal confrontation is necessary. Peace returns more quickly if I do not try to deny my aggressive emotions.

  Later when my angry emotions have calmed, I may ask myself what frightens *me* about the other person's behavior. But I do not turn to this perspective until my anger has subsided, because I do not wish to suppress my anger prematurely. Suppression of anger before it has run its course leads to depression.

At the beginning and end of formal meditation repeat this exercise over several breath cycles: *My angry thoughts and feelings prevent me from seeing a meaningful world.*

Now, when you are ready, begin formal meditation.

First find a comfortable straight back chair. Sit erect in the chair with both feet planted on the floor. Put your hands on your legs or fold them in your lap. Breathe through your nose when you can. Close your eyes and notice your abdomen expand as you say "in" to yourself.

Notice your abdomen contract as you say "out." Feel at peace as you follow your breath.

1. After meditation write on a card: *My angry thoughts and feelings prevent me from seeing a meaningful world*. During the day at frequent intervals look at the card and each time be still for a moment. When you are still, follow your breath, "in" and "out" as your abdomen rises and falls with your breath through several cycles. Be at peace.

At the end of the day record one example of using this or any exercise to acknowledge and process your angry thoughts and feelings. Remember your Disruptions Notebook.

2. In the last minutes of formal meditation search for someone you will encounter today toward whom you are likely to feel angry. Write notes in your mind to one person who irritates you and rebuke him for his errors. Then put yourself in the other person's shoes. Imagine him receiving your letter and being contrite. Then imagine a letter of apology from this thoroughly rebuked person, and in the letter, have the rebuked one admit the *fears* that led him to act in a frightened way.

Finally, imagine your letter of forgiveness.

At the very end of the meditation see clearly in your mind the picture of your goal, in addition to peace of mind, for these eight weeks. Hold that picture. Notice the details. Feel at peace with that picture.

After meditation, write this exercise on a card or piece of paper that you will look at several times today: *My angry thoughts and feelings prevent me from seeing a meaningful world*. Look at the exercise during the day and whenever you do be still for a moment. When you are still, follow your breath, "in" and "out" as your abdomen rises and falls. Follow your breath through several cycles. Be at peace.

At the end of the day write in your journal one example of using this or any exercise to achieve a shift in perception that brought with it peace of mind. Remember your Disruptions Notebook.

3. This time add the warm bright light to the process. In the last minutes of formal meditation, after using the lesson to process your angry thoughts and feelings, let the warm, bright light build in you. First feel a warm bright light in the middle of your body and in your heart. Then when the warmth fills your heart let it expand to all your body. When you are thoroughly warmed by the light, let it flow from you to an image of the other person and envelop him in the warm bright light of kindness and compassion.

At the very end of the meditation see clearly in your mind the picture of your goal, in addition to peace of mind, for these eight weeks. Hold that picture. Notice the details. Feel at peace with that picture.

After meditation, write this exercise on a card or piece of paper that you will look at several times today: *My angry thoughts and feelings prevent me from seeing a meaningful world*. Look at the exercise during the day and be still for a moment each time you do. When you are still, follow your breath, "in" and "out" as your abdomen rises and falls. Follow your breath through several cycles. Be at peace.

At the end of the day write in your journal one example of using this or any exercise to achieve a shift in perception that brought with it peace of mind. Remember your Disruptions Notebook.

EXERCISE 5

HURT IS HATE DIRECTED AT MYSELF.[34]

Remember that earlier we considered hurt and hate as normal emotions, not emotions that we need to judge harshly. Rather, they may be opportunities or signposts that direct us to areas where renewal might take place. Here is one way to process hurt:

1. Recognize that hurt is disguised anger at someone else.
2. Turn the direction of the feeling around by feeling anger at that person.
3. Stay with the feeling of hate until, like a storm, it passes.
4. Acknowledge your willingness to forgive.
5. Ask the force to help you forgive the other person.
6. *Ask yourself, "Why does this person's behavior frighten me?"*

In my psychiatry residency my psychotherapy supervisor missed his first appointment with me and then the second one, as well. I was distraught, injured, rejected, and abused. What I did not feel was that I wished to strangle that jerk for keeping me in his waiting room twice in a row without so much as an "I'm sorry." Had I been able to feel angry at him, I would not have felt so hurt. But I was afraid to feel angry because I was afraid I might show my feelings. I was afraid if I showed my feelings he would dismiss me as a psychiatrist and my career would be ruined.

Later, when I was bumbling in supervision with him,

he suggested that I might not know that I was still as angry with him as I should be for his not showing up for my first two supervisions. I learned subsequently that he was right, but at the time I could not admit it to myself. Finally I discovered that he hadn't shown up for those first sessions because he had been trying to help the authorities deal with the civil rights disturbances of that period. But what about my reaction of being too afraid to feel my anger toward him? What was that all about?

I experienced him as the only person I could turn to in the maze of my early residency training. Of course, that was not true. As a matter of fact, I soon arranged excellent supervision with Marvin Starman, a person I still remain close to. So I was experiencing my supervisor more as I might have experienced my mother when I was small and she was truly the only person who could gratify me. That was why I was so afraid of alienating him. I had to feel hurt rather than hate. Now it should be safe to turn around feelings of hurt and to discover the feelings of hate that stimulate them, because I do not have to show my feelings. I can work them out in my mind, rather than in action.

Today I can open myself to hurt feelings and process them to acknowledge my hate, then fearfulness.

At the beginning and end of formal meditation repeat this exercise over several breath cycles: *Hurt is hate directed at myself.*

Now when you are ready, begin formal meditation.

First find a comfortable straight back chair. Sit erect in the chair with both feet planted on the floor. Put your hands on your legs or fold them in your lap. Breathe through your nose when you can. Close your eyes and notice your abdomen expand as you say "in" to yourself. Notice your abdomen contract as you say "out." Feel at peace as you follow your breath.

1. After meditation write this exercise on a card or piece of paper that you will look at several times today: *Hurt is hate directed at myself.* Look at the exercise during the day and be still for a moment each time you do. When you are still, follow your breath, "in" and "out" as your abdomen rises and falls with your breath. Follow your breath through several cycles. Be at peace.

At the end of the day write in your journal one example of using this or any exercise to achieve a shift in perception that brought with it peace of mind. Remember your Disruptions Notebook.

2. In the last few minutes of formal meditation anticipate a situation in your life today when you might feel hurt. Imagine yourself feeling hurt first, then turn the vector of aggression outward and feel hate toward the person. Ask yourself, "Is this person a stand-in for someone in my childhood story?" Then, pay attention to whomever comes into your mind. Feel hate toward that person, too. When the waves of feeling pass, return to your breath and feel peace of mind that comes with acknowledging a willingness to forgive. As a final step ask yourself, "What frightens me here?" Pay attention to whatever comes to mind, because that will be the answer to your question.

At the very end of the meditation see clearly in your mind the picture of your goal, in addition to peace of mind, for these eight weeks. Hold that picture. Notice the details. Feel at peace with that picture.

After meditation, write this exercise on a card or piece of paper that you will look at several times today: *Hurt is hate directed at myself*. Look at the exercise during the day and be still for a moment each time you do. When you are still, follow your breath, "in" and "out" as your abdomen rises and falls with your breath. Follow your breath through several cycles. Be at peace.

At the end of the day write in your journal one example of using this or any exercise to achieve a shift in perception that brought with it peace of mind. Remember your Disruptions Notebook.

3. Think of someone in your past who hurt you. Hate that person. When the storm of feelings passes, ask yourself, "What frightened me here?" Acknowledge a willingness to forgive. Finish the process by invoking the warm, bright light to join with the person in the past who hurt your feelings. First feel a warm bright light in the middle of your body, in your heart. Then when the warmth fills your heart let it expand to all your body. Then when you are thoroughly warmed by the light, let it flow from you to an image of the other person and envelop it in the warm bright light of kindness and compassion. This person had a lesson to teach you; see if you can identify it.

At the very end of the meditation see clearly in your mind the picture of your goal, in addition to peace of mind, for these eight weeks. Hold that picture. Notice the details. Feel at peace with that picture.

After meditation, write this exercise on a card or piece of paper that you will look at several times today: *Hurt is hate directed at myself*. Look at the exercise during the day and be still for a moment each time you do. When you are still, follow your breath, "in" and "out" as your abdomen rises and falls with your breath. Follow your breath through several cycles. Be at peace.

At the end of the day write in your journal one example of using this or any exercise to achieve a shift in perception that brought with it peace of mind. Remember your Disruptions Notebook.

EXERCISE 6

LISTENING IS LOVE IN ACTION.[35]

When I was in medical school I had a classmate named Tom. Tom was the youngest of our group, but he was an advanced listener. Many of the older medical students sought Tom's company because he was able to connect with them by listening intently without trying to change the subject or suggesting different ways to see things. Tom did not attempt to teach lessons or interpret what he heard, he just listened. I was amazed that he could do that. I found myself, by contrast, trying to counsel, to give alternative ways of looking at things, often before I had heard the other person out. Tom rarely made this mistake. He was a great teacher to me.

Listening intently is to get more detail, to let every opportunity for interaction be a chance for a connection. Three steps to good listening are as follows: accepting, acknowledging, and joining. Accepting means not judging. Acknowledging means to restate what you have heard, if only to yourself. Joining means remembering similar experiences that you have had. You don't have to tell similar experiences; often just remembering them is enough. Even a chance meeting on an elevator can provide the opportunity for connection if we are open and listen carefully.

At the beginning and end of formal meditation repeat this exercise over several breath cycles: *Listening is love in action.*

Now, if you feel ready, begin formal meditation.

First find a comfortable straight back chair. Sit erect in the chair with both feet planted on the floor. Put your hands on your legs or fold them in your lap. Breathe through your nose when you can. Close your eyes and notice your abdomen expand as you say "in" to yourself. Notice your abdomen contract as you say "out." Feel at peace as you follow your breath.

1. After meditation, write this exercise on a card or piece of paper that you will look at several times today: *Listening is love in action.* Look at the exercise during the day and be still for a moment each time you do. When you are still, follow your breath, "in" and "out" as your abdomen rises and falls with your breath. Follow your breath through several cycles. Be at peace.

At the end of the day write in your journal one example of using this or any exercise to achieve a shift in perception that brought with it peace of mind. Remember your Disruptions Notebook.

2. In the last few minutes of formal meditation think of someone you might encounter today who usually stimulates in you a desire to react, rather than to listen. Plan in advance a period of careful listening to that person. Write the occurrence of that encounter or lack of it in your journal at the end of the day.

At the very end of the meditation see clearly in your mind the picture of your goal, in addition to peace of mind, for these eight weeks. Hold that picture. Notice the details. Feel at peace with that picture.

After meditation write this exercise on a card or piece of paper that you will look at several times today: *Listening is love in action.* Look at the exercise during the day and be still for a moment each time you do. When you are still, follow your breath, "in" and "out" as your abdomen rises and falls with your breath. Follow your breath through several cycles. Be at peace.

At the end of the day write in your journal one example of using this or any exercise to achieve a shift in perception that brought with it peace of mind. Remember your Disruptions Notebook.

3. Think of a person in your past to whom you reacted rather than listened. Feel the full force of any aggressive emotion toward that person. When the storm of feelings passes, imagine joining with that person through the use of your warm, bright light. First feel a warm bright light in the middle of your body, in your heart. Then when the warmth fills your heart let it expand to all your body. When you are thoroughly warmed by the light, let it flow from you to an image of the other person and envelop her in the warm bright light of kindness and compassion.

At the very end of the meditation see clearly in your mind the picture of your goal, in addition to peace of mind, for these eight weeks. Hold that picture. Notice the details. Feel at peace with that picture.

After meditation write this exercise on a card or piece of paper that you will look at several times today: *Listening is love in action*. Look at the exercise during the day and be still for a moment each time you do. When you are still, follow your breath, "in" and "out" as your abdomen rises and falls with your breath. Follow your breath through several cycles. Be at peace.

At the end of the day write in your journal one example of using this or any exercise to achieve a shift in perception that brought with it peace of mind. Remember your Disruptions Notebook.

EXERCISE 7

DO I WANT TO BE RIGHT, OR DO I WANT PEACE OF MIND?[36]

Pyrrhus, king of Epirus, defeated the Romans at Asculum in 279 B.C. at an enormous cost of his soldiers' lives. He reportedly said: "One more such victory over the Romans, and we are utterly undone." Hence the term "Pyrrhic victory" has come down through the years. When I fight a battle rather than waging peace, I suffer heavy losses, even if I win.

When I was in high school in South Carolina, I spent summers in Michigan with my grandparents. I heard some of the local fishermen telling stories about smelt, of how these little fish came down the streams, overflowed the banks, and could be then scooped up. When I went home at the end of summer, I told my friends stories of these little fish swarming like bees and they scoffed at me. One day they were teasing me in biology class where the teacher, Mr. Hubbard, listened with equal skepticism. Incensed, I set about proving my smelt story. I gathered *National Geographic* articles, encyclopedia references, and many *Field and Stream* magazines. I lay waste the opposition in a torrent of information that was too formidable to deny. I spent so much time systematically proving my smelt stories that Mr. Hubbard referred to me as "Smelt" for the rest of the year. He did this with characteristic good humor and in a way that made me feel recognized rather than put down.

The original teasing was all in fun, but I had made a federal case of it. If I met Mr. Hubbard today he would probably call me "Smelt." He might have a point. My insis-

tence on being right grew old after a while, and I alienated others by my pugnacity. So today, with the help of
the force, I choose peace over Pyrrhic victories.

At the beginning and end of formal meditation repeat
this exercise over several breath cycles: *Do I want to be
right or do I want peace of mind?*

Now, when you are ready, begin formal meditation.

First find a comfortable straight back chair. Sit erect
in the chair with both feet planted on the floor. Put your
hands on your legs or fold them in your lap. Breathe
through your nose when you can. Close your eyes and
notice your abdomen expand as you say "in" to yourself.
Notice your abdomen contract as you say "out." Feel at
peace as you follow your breath.

1. After meditation, write this exercise on a card or
piece of paper that you will look at several times today:
Do I want to be right or do I want peace of mind? Look at
the exercise during the day and be still for a moment each
time you do. When you are still, follow your breath, "in"
and "out" as your abdomen rises and falls with your
breath. Follow your breath through several cycles. Be at
peace.

At the end of the day write in your journal one example of using this or any exercise to achieve a shift in perception that brought with it epace of mind. Remember
your Disruptions Notebook.

2. In the last few minutes of formal meditation think
of a person you know you will encounter today with whom
you will be tempted to do verbal battle. Imagine waging
peace through careful listening rather than waging war.

At the very end of the meditation see clearly in your

mind the picture of your goal, in addition to peace of mind, for these eight weeks. Hold that picture. Notice the details. Feel at peace with that picture.

After meditation write this exercise on a card or piece of paper that you will look at several times today: *Do I want to be right or do I want peace of mind?* Look at the exercise during the day and be still for a moment each time you do. When you are still, follow your breath "in" and "out" as your abdomen rises and falls. Follow your breath through several cycles. Be at peace.

At the end of the day write in your journal one example of using this or any exercise to achieve a shift in perception that brought with it peace of mind. Remember your Disruptions Notebook.

3. In the last few minutes of formal meditation remember a person from your past you tended to react to by one-upmanship. If you feel guilty about the way you treated her, feel the guilt until the storm of feelings passes. Then, remember that errors are for correction, not for unending suffering in guilt.

Imagine dropping the issues you tended to ague about and making peace with that person through bright-light joining. First feel a warm bright light in the middle of your body, in your heart. Then when the warmth fills your heart let it expand to all your body and when you are thoroughly warmed, let it flow from you to an image of the other person and envelop her in the warm bright light of kindness and compassion.

At the very end of the meditation see clearly in your mind the picture of your goal, in addition to peace of mind, for these eight weeks. Hold that picture. Notice the details. Feel at peace with that picture.

After meditation write this exercise on a card or piece of paper that you will look at several times today: *Do I want to be right or do I want peace of mind?* Look at the exercise during the day and be still for a moment each time you do. When you are still, follow your breath "in" and "out" as your abdomen rises and falls. Follow your breath through several cycles. Be at peace.

At the end of the day write in your journal one example of using this or any exercise to achieve a shift in perception that brought with it peace of mind. Remember your Disruptions Notebook.

WEEK 3

My Childhood Story Distorts My Adult Experience

This week we will be extending the work we began in the first week by attempting to assess the impact of childhood on adult perceptions. One guide to the eruption of our story into adult life is the experience of *a sense of urgency*. Whenever we experience an *urgency to act*, whenever we notice that we are in a *hurry*, chances are that our immediate experience is being colored by some version of our childhood story.

In addition to reading the lessons, meditating and journaling each day, remember to write in your Disruptions Notebook any major interruptions to your peace of mind. Be sure to describe the persons whom you find disruptive in as much detail as possible. This detail will be important when you use this notebook to map the characters in your story later in the lessons. Also important are the fears you experience, so write them down in as much detail as possible.

MY STORY DISRUPTS MY PEACE OF MIND.[37]

The first time I had a manuscript accepted for publication, I dreamt that I was chained to my word processor. I remembered that in Dante's *Divine Comedy,* a person's hell was related to the way he lived his life. I imagined myself stuck in front of the word processor for all eternity and I had fantasies of dying. I told my wife, Renée, about my dream and described the fears I was experiencing. She helped me figure them out.

I remembered my earliest childhood nightmare where I had something to type, but I was only 3 and could not type. When I touched the keys of the typewriter they made a loud sound like a gunshot. When I heard that my first manuscript was going to be published, I worried that I would not be able to rewrite the parts that needed it, despite the fact that I could write well enough at the time.

At the time of my childhood nightmare, I was alone with my mother. My father was on a ship in the Pacific and I was the man of the house. My mother admired me for what I could read when all I had done was memorize a few words in my kiddy books. I could not read the newspaper like a real man. I was not old enough to be man of the house, and if I tried to be I imagined my father would hate me. I imagined that he might even want to kill me. I was terrified and it was made worse by not being able to communicate what it was that frightened me so.

In retrospect I knew my father was away fighting in the war; I knew he might be killed. I suppose it must have occurred to me that if he were killed I could have my mother all to myself. The wish that he be killed in the war scared me. What would I do then? I could not even type. How would I ever be the man of the house?

As Renée and I were working on my dream together, I remembered that when I had my nightmare in childhood I was afraid of loud noises. Loud noises reminded me of the stories my father told me about the war when he was home on leave. At that age when I went to Western movies, I cringed at the sound of gunshots. They sent shivers all through me as if someone was really being hurt. I speculate now that I did not want to be reminded that I had imagined my father being killed in the war so I would have my mother all to myself.

My mother admired writers, especially writers of books like *The Little Engine That Could*. When I heard that my first paper would be published, I reexperienced all my childhood fears when I dreamed that I could impress my mother by writing a book on the typewriter. At the same time I feared that such success might be accompanied by my father's death, which would expose me to the humiliation of not really being man enough to take care of my mother.

It may seem far-fetched that a little boy would think that he could kill his father with his wishes, but I remember my older son, Michael, coming to me in tears because he shot a man on television with his toy gun and at the same time the man fell off his horse, dead. That coincidence convinced Michael that his play wishes were really lethal. Not long after that I came home from work one day and Michael threw his arms around me. "What did I do to deserve the big hug?" I asked. "I'm glad you're all right," he said. "Why of course I am. Why wouldn't I be?" I said.

He looked sheepish for a moment and said faintly, "Because I shot you in my imagination."

Children worry that their wishes are capable of making things happen in a magical way. Adults are not free of these fears either.

Today when I feel a sense of urgency or fear, I try to examine what in my childhood might be peeking into my adult life.

At the beginning and end of formal meditation repeat this exercise over several breath cycles: *My story disrupts my peace of mind.* Now, when you are ready, begin formal meditation.

Sit erect in your comfortable straight back chair with both feet planted on the floor. Put your hands on your legs or fold them in your lap. Breathe through your nose when you can. Close your eyes and notice your abdomen expand as you say "in" to yourself; notice your abdomen contract as you say "out." Feel at peace as you follow your breath.

1. After meditation write this exercise on a card or piece of paper that you will look at several times today: *My story disrupts my peace of mind.* Look at the exercise during the day and be still for a moment each time you do.

At the end of the day write in your journal one example of using this or any exercise to achieve a shift in perception that brought with it peace of mind. Remember your Disruptions Notebook.

2. In the last few minutes of formal meditation imagine someone you are likely to treat as a part of your childhood story in your life today, someone whom you have urgent need to please or get praise or recognition from.

Imagine a disappointing meeting with that person and how you might deal with it emotionally to achieve peace of mind.

At the very end of the meditation see clearly in your mind the picture of your goal, in addition to peace of mind, for these eight weeks. Hold that picture. Notice the details. Feel at peace with that picture.

After meditation, write this exercise on a card or piece of paper that you will look at several times today: *My story disrupts my peace of mind.* Look at the exercise during the day and be still for a moment each time you do.

At the end of the day write in your journal one example of using this or any exercise to achieve a shift in perception that brought with it peace of mind. Remember your Disruptions Notebook.

3. In the final minutes of formal meditation imagine a person from your remote past for whom you harbor resentment and bitterness. Let yourself feel the full force of these feelings for as long as they last. When the storm quiets, let the warm, bright light build in you. Let it build in your heart. When you can feel it there, let it spread to the rest of your body. Let yourself really feel the bright light within you before you let it spread to another. Then let it join you to the other person.

At the very end of the meditation see clearly in your mind the picture of your goal, in addition to peace of mind, for these eight weeks. Hold that picture. Notice the details. Feel at peace with that picture.

After meditation, write this exercise on a card or piece of paper that you will look at several times today: *My story disrupts my peace of mind.* Look at the exercise during the day and be still for a moment each time you do.

At the end of the day write in your journal one example of using this or any exercise to achieve a shift in perception that brought with it peace of mind. Remember your Disruptions Notebook.

MY STORY IS REPEATED IN MY
SCRIPTS FOR OTHER PEOPLE.

One disadvantage to having *The Little Engine That Could* play such a big role in my life is that I expect everyone else to operate with similar determination, even when determination might not be the optimal mode, such as in times of grief. When someone loses a loved one, it is better to let the grief be there than to try to go about business as usual. Even in smaller occurrences expecting too much initiative and determination can be a problem.

For example, if I come home from work and Renée mentions that a porch light has burned out, my immediate reaction is to feel annoyed that she did not replace it. Why doesn't she show more initiative? When my son got a low grade in school, I might expect that he would see this temporary setback as an opportunity to show his determination to do better, right? Not always. What a rude awakening it was to learn that some important people in my life were operating under the influence of their childhood stories. Tom Sawyer in *Huckleberry Finn* was a more operative character in my son's life at times than *The Little Engine That Could.* I learned an important lesson: whenever I invest too much in the outcome of someone else's behavior with my own sense of urgency, I am experiencing the latest episode of my story. My story can easily be imposed on others as a script or a set routine I expect from another person. A script contains the belief that if the other person does not do his role just right, then I cannot be happy.

With a son in the sixth grade I may be operating from "I think I can, I think I can," when he is really more influenced by "Hazy, Lazy Days of Summer." I have a chance to be helpful only if I recognize that it is more useful to learn more about the other person's experiences, thoughts, and feelings than it is to rush in to "fix" them.

At the beginning and end of formal meditation repeat this exercise over several breath cycles: *My story is repeated in my scripts for other people.*

Now, when you are ready, begin formal meditation.

Sit erect in your comfortable straight back chair with both feet planted on the floor. Put your hands on your legs or fold them in your lap. Breathe through your nose when you can. Close your eyes and notice your abdomen expand as you say "in" and contract as you say "out." Feel at peace as you follow your breath.

1. After meditation write this exercise on a card or piece of paper that you will look at several times today: *My story is repeated in my scripts for other people.* Look at the exercise during the day and be still for a moment each time you do.

At the end of the day write in your journal one example of using this or any exercise to achieve a shift in perception that brought with it peace of mind. Remember your Disruptions Notebook.

2. In the last few minutes of formal meditation find a person in your life right now in whom you have an investment in the outcome of his or her actions. Imagine that desire being thwarted. Imagine your acknowledging your disappointment with dignity and serenity.

At the very end of the meditation see clearly in your mind the picture of your goal, in addition to peace of mind, for these eight weeks. Hold that picture. Notice the details. Feel at peace with that picture.

After formal meditation, write this exercise on a card or piece of paper that you will look at several times today: *My story is repeated in my scripts for other people.* Look at the exercise during the day and be still for a moment each time you do.

At the end of the day write in your journal one example of using this or any exercise to achieve a shift in perception that brought with it peace of mind. Remember your Disruptions Notebook.

3. In the last few minutes of formal meditation remember a person in your remote past who disappointed you. Feel the disappointment and feel the anger. When the strong aggressive emotions pass, acknowledge how they failed to play the role you wished for in your script. When you feel ready, let the warm, bright light build in your heart. Allow that warmth and brightness to flow throughout your body and then to the one who disappointed you.

At the very end of the meditation see clearly in your mind the picture of your goal, in addition to peace of mind, for these eight weeks. Hold that picture. Notice the details. Feel at peace with that picture.

After meditation write this exercise on a card or piece of paper that you will look at several times today: *My story is repeated in my scripts for other people.* Look at the exercise during the day and be still for a moment each time you do. When you are still, follow your breath, "in" and "out" as your abdomen rises and falls with your breath. Follow your breath through several cycles and be at peace.

At the end of the day write in your journal one example of using this or any exercise to achieve a shift in perception that brought with it peace of mind. Remember your Disruptions Notebook.

Exercise 3

I WILL GIVE UP MY SCRIPTS
FOR OTHER PEOPLE.[38]

I know that I learned to deal with my friends, family, and colleagues by having a role in mind for each to play in my life's story. To paraphrase Oscar Wilde: To be truly selfish is not to live one's life the way one wishes but to try to get others to live their lives the way one wishes.

I want my friend, Jim, to think of me first when lining up golf or tennis. I want my daughter-in-law to have children so I might have the pleasure of being a grandfather. I want my wife to enjoy the same movies I do. I want her to want sex whenever I do. I try to get others to fit the role I've assigned them to play in my life.

This is a self-centered way to view the world, but I do it because the egocentric illusion of childhood is present in me all the time. I still wish, in the recesses of my mind, that the world revolved around me. So I recognize that this wish will always be alive in my mind, but I do not have to put it into action. In my actions I can have a choice.

Today I will make a special effort to recognize when I am trying to get someone to play a part in my story and I will release him to be himself. I will use as a guide to these moments times when I feel *tension* when dealing with another person.

At the beginning and end of formal meditation repeat this exercise over several breath cycles: *I will give up my scripts for other people*. Now, when you are ready, begin formal meditation.

Sit erect in your comfortable straight back chair with both feet planted on the floor. Put your hands on your legs

or fold them in your lap. Breathe through your nose when you can. Close your eyes and notice your abdomen expand as you say "in" and contract as you say "out." Feel at peace as you follow your breath.

1. After meditation, write this exercise on a card or piece of paper that you will look at several times today: *I will give up my scripts for other people.* Look at the exercise during the day and be still for a moment each time you do.

At the end of the day write in your journal one example of using this or any exercise to achieve a shift in perception that brought with it peace of mind. Remember your Disruptions Notebook.

2. In the last few minutes of formal meditation anticipate an interaction with someone today whom you wish to have a role in your scripts. Think of the situation and imagine how you'll feel if that person refuses to be a participant. Stay with the strong feelings until they pass. Then imagine feeling peace as you let go of your expectations for this person.

At the very end of the meditation see clearly in your mind the picture of your goal, in addition to peace of mind, for these eight weeks. Hold that picture. Notice the details. Feel at peace with that picture.

After meditation, write this exercise on a card or piece of paper that you will look at several times today: *I will give up my scripts for other people.* Look at the exercise during the day and be still for a moment each time you do. When you are still, follow your breath, "in" and "out" as your abdomen rises and falls with your breath. Follow your breath through several cycles. Be at peace.

At the end of the day write in your journal one example of using this or any exercise to achieve a shift in perception that brought with it peace of mind. Remember your Disruptions Notebook.

3. In the last few minutes of formal meditation let yourself feel the full strength of your wishes toward someone in the past. Remember how you wanted that person to act. Let yourself feel really angry at her or him for disappointing you. After your angry feelings quiet, step back emotionally and acknowledge that you do not know what is in your best interest. Imagine how that person's actions may have taught you a valuable lesson. Then let a bright light form within you; let it build in your heart and spread throughout your body. Let it spread to the person whom you wanted to play a role in your story. Release that person with warmth.

At the very end of the meditation see clearly in your mind the picture of your goal, in addition to peace of mind, for these eight weeks. Hold that picture. Notice the details. Feel at peace with that picture.

After meditation write this exercise on a card or piece of paper that you will look at several times today: *I will give up my scripts for other people.* Look at the exercise during the day and be still for a moment each time you do. When you are still, follow your breath, "in" and "out" as your abdomen rises and falls with your breath. Follow your breath through several cycles. Be at peace.

At the end of the day write in your journal one example of using this or any exercise to achieve a shift in perception that brought with it peace of mind. Remember your Disruptions Notebook.

THE WORLD I SEE DOES NOT
VICTIMIZE ME.[39]

There are times that I feel victimized by the happenings
and the people around me. Often this is a sign that I harbor hate toward the persons I imagine are giving me a hard
time. This is the time for recapturing those hateful feelings and directing them toward the others rather than
feeling on the receiving end of them. Once I have been able
to turn around the vector of aggression, then I can write
a letter of accusation in my mind, receive a letter of apology, and return a letter of forgiveness. With some practice I can do this with lightning speed in my imagination.

   I can also find people in my past who disappointed
me in similar ways. I will not forget the past, because all
my *urgent* feelings in the present receive contributions
from the past. But I may have to *accept* my strong feelings toward people in the past before I can see the present
more clearly. Included in seeing the present more clearly
is accepting what frightens me about another's behavior.

   Earlier I mentioned that when I was quite young and
I convinced my mother to buy me that model airplane, I
really felt victimized. The airplane looked great on the
package, but inside it was just balsa sticks and paper. I
could not figure out how this went together to make a
model; I was stuck. My mother could not figure it out
either; we were both stuck. I was sure that if my father
were home, he would know what to do with the sticks to
make an airplane out of them. But he was not home; he
was at war. I felt angry and betrayed. I was certain that
I had been cheated by the store and by my mother who

did not want to confront the salesperson with evidence of his treachery.

When I was 15, I tried my hand again at the same model airplane, an F–4U Corsair and this time I made it. I felt especially proud of doing something that had once stumped me. I had not known or could not accept that it would take some maturation and development before I could put together a model airplane.

Today, if I am faced with a challenge that I have not met before, I fear that I will reexperience the model airplane all over again. The model-airplane-incident and the herd-of-cows-in-the-backyard incident speak first whenever I try something new. My frightened-self speaks first.

At the beginning and end of formal meditation repeat this exercise over several breath cycles: *The world I see does not victimize me.*

Now, when you are ready, begin formal meditation.

Sit erect in your comfortable straight back chair with both feet planted on the floor. Put your hands on your legs or fold them in your lap. Breathe through your nose when you can. Close your eyes and notice your abdomen expand as you say "in" and contract as you say "out." Feel at peace as you follow your breath.

1. After meditation write this exercise on a card or piece of paper that you will look at several times today: *The world I see does not victimize me.* Look at the exercise during the day and be still for a moment each time you do. When you are still, follow your breath, "in" and "out" as your abdomen rises and falls with your breath. Follow your breath through several cycles. Be at peace.

At the end of the day write in your journal one example of using this or any exercise to achieve a shift in per-

ception that brought with it peace of mind. Remember your Disruptions Notebook.

2. In the last few minutes of formal meditation search your memories for anyone in your present life who is likely to stimulate feelings of victimization in you. If you find someone, anticipate dealing with that person using this lesson. If no one in the present seems likely to affect you this way, remember the last time you felt like a victim and process that experience using this lesson.

At the very end of the meditation see clearly in your mind the picture of your goal, in addition to peace of mind, for these eight weeks. Hold that picture. Notice the details. Feel at peace with that picture.

After meditation write this exercise on a card or piece of paper that you will look at several times today: *The world I see does not victimize me.* Look at the exercise during the day and be still for a moment each time you do.

At the end of the day write in your journal one example of using this or any exercise to achieve a shift in perception that brought with it peace of mind. Remember your Disruptions Notebook.

3. In the last few minutes of formal meditation remember someone from the past who made you feel like a victim. Feel all the hate and anger you can feel toward this person until the storm subsides. Then feel the warm, bright light build in your heart and let the warmth spread within you. When you feel ready, allow the bright light to envelop one person you previously experienced as a persecutor.

At the very end of the meditation see clearly in your mind the picture of your goal, in addition to peace of mind,

for these eight weeks. Hold that picture. Notice the details. Feel at peace with that picture.

After meditation write this exercise on a card or piece of paper that you will look at several times today: *The world I see does not victimize me.* Look at the exercise during the day and be still for a moment each time you do. When you are still, follow your breath, "in" and "out" as your abdomen rises and falls with your breath. Follow your breath through several cycles. Be at peace.

At the end of the day write in your journal one example of using this or any exercise to achieve a shift in perception that brought with it peace of mind. Remember your Disruptions Notebook.

THAT WHICH SUFFERS IS
NOT REALLY ME.[40]

A crucial step in recognizing my story is recognizing that whatever suffers is not really me. My story is the drama I play out when I am feeling hurt or angry. I learned to play a particular role as a child in order to fit into someone else's world. Whenever I feel the beginning of suffering, I can ask myself, "Who is this person?" Chances are that I learned to play the suffering role from someone in my family. I can uncover this unwanted imitation by being still for a moment and asking the question, "Who is this person?" Then I will rebuke and forgive that person for teaching me this role.

After medical school I went to Detroit to do my internship and residency. Renée and I were lucky enough to find an apartment over a garage in a suburb of Detroit. We were tipped off about it by a family member who thought that it was available, but the family was not advertising its availability. Were we ever surprised! This was no ordinary apartment but one over an eight-car garage. It had three bedrooms, three bathrooms, and a living-dining room that was 40 by 60 feet. But there was one problem. In the middle of that room was a pool table. Not that it wasn't a beautiful pool table, but right in the middle of the room was too much. The owners did not mind if we moved the table, so we planned to move it to a storage area.

Then it occurred to us that there was no opening in this room big enough for the table to be moved through. We consulted a man who had helped with the original construction of the room and he assured us that there was a way to get the table out. We could reverse the process of moving it in. It had been moved in by crane before the roof was put on. As accommodating as our landlords were, Renée and I doubted that they would go for removing the roof.

At first I felt defeated. In the midst of this huge area I was suffering. All I could think of was the unhealthy social consequences of my sons being raised in a pool hall. By the time they were 5 they would probably have turned to beer. Then what? Heaven knows! My reaction was clearly out of proportion to the problem. Rather than looking at our good fortune, all I could think about was that blasted pool table. Renée was more realistic. She said, "We will work around it." And that is exactly what we did. Looking back on it, I wish I had known to ask myself, "Who is this person who focuses on the one problem rather than enjoying the terrific place to live?" If I had I would have known immediately: Aunt Emily.

My Aunt Emily liked nothing better than to regale me with the injustices done to her, while she was only trying to be helpful to others. She seemed to experience her life as if no blessing were without a much larger hidden curse. As a child when I was with her, I remember slanting stories toward a similar theme, just to fit in. It is not a useful imitation to me now, although it served me well as a way to connect with Aunt Emily when I was younger. It probably served a similar purpose for her when she was a little girl.

The ghost of Aunt Emily did not prevail in the case of the apartment and the pool table, because Renée was not inclined to manufacture misery. We did not move the pool table at all. Renée turned the pool table into a centerpiece that served the following purposes:

1. My children and I learned to play pool.
2. In the winter, the children used it as the infield of the race track they ran their peddle cars around.
3. With a pad on the table, an electric train set ran without fear of derailing because the train track was close to the pool rail.
4. Holiday meals were served from a buffet that perched atop the plywood cover and tablecloths that we used to transform it into a perfect banquet table.
5. With the addition of a foam rubber pallet, it became a perfect bed for the children of guests, in effect a fourth bedroom.

When we left the area for me to serve in the military following the completion of my residency, we moved into a town-house near Bethesda Naval Hospital. We missed that big room and the pool table. By relinquishing my suffering role, I had made friends with what had seemed a barrier to peace.

Does relinquishing my suffering mean that I can escape painful feelings? Not in this life. No matter how good I get at relinquishing my suffering role, there will always be moments of sadness, depression, loneliness, disappointment, and other normal and useful feelings. I can use these feelings for further growth by acknowledging them and, with the help of the force, using them as guideposts to those lessons I need to learn.

At the beginning and end of formal meditation repeat this exercise over several breath cycles: *That which suffers is not really me.*

Now, when you are ready, begin formal meditation.

Sit erect in your comfortable straight back chair with both feet planted on the floor. Put your hands on your legs

or fold them in your lap. Breathe through your nose when you can. Close your eyes and notice your abdomen expand as you say "in" and contract as you say "out." Feel at peace as you follow your breath.

1. After meditation write this exercise on a card or piece of paper that you will look at several times today: *That which suffers is not really me.* Look at the exercise during the day and be still for a moment each time you do. When you are still, follow your breath, "in" and "out" as your abdomen rises and falls with your breath. Follow your breath through several cycles. Be at peace.

At the end of the day write in your journal one example of using this or any exercise to achieve a shift in perception that brought with it peace of mind. Remember your Disruptions Notebook.

2. In the last few minutes of formal meditation take a few extra moments to think ahead into your day. Imagine a situation that is likely to occur in which you might be tempted to suffer. Ask yourself whom you would be imitating if you did choose to suffer. Imagine handling the situation without suffering but with dignity and grace.

At the very end of the meditation see clearly in your mind the picture of your goal, in addition to peace of mind, for these eight weeks. Hold that picture. Notice the details. Feel at peace with that picture.

After meditation write this exercise on a card or piece of paper that you will look at several times today: *That which suffers is not really me.* Look at the exercise during the day and be still for a moment each time you do. When you are still, follow your breath, "in" and "out" as your abdomen rises and falls with your breath. Follow your breath through several cycles. Be at peace.

At the end of the day write in your journal one example of using this or any exercise to achieve a shift in perception that brought with it peace of mind. Remember your Disruptions Notebook.

3. At the end of formal meditation, remember a situation in your past when you suffered. Ask yourself whom you were imitating. Feel the force of your anger at this person for teaching you this role. Then when the storm passes, be still for a moment, let the bright light develop in your heart. After you feel the warmth for a while, let the light and warmth spread to the rest of your body. When you feel ready, let it spread to the person who taught you the suffering role.

At the very end of the meditation see clearly in your mind the picture of your goal, in addition to peace of mind, for these eight weeks. Hold that picture. Notice the details. Feel at peace with that picture.

After meditation write this exercise on a card or piece of paper that you will look at several times today: *That which suffers is not really me.* Look at the exercise during the day and be still for a moment each time you do. When you are still, follow your breath, "in" and "out" as your abdomen rises and falls with your breath. Follow your breath through several cycles. Be at peace.

At the end of the day write in your journal one example of using this or any exercise to achieve a shift in perception that brought with it peace of mind. Remember the Disruptions Notebook.

EXERCISE 6

ATTACHMENTS ARE PART OF MY STORY.[41]

For me, attachments fall into three major categories: (1) attachments to outcomes, (2) attachments to things, and (3) attachment to being right. I remember thinking in high school that I could not live if the girl of my dreams did not reciprocate my affection. I remember thinking that the outcome of each football game was the most important thing that could happen in the world. I remember wanting to have my own column in the school newspaper and feeling as though my life depended on it. The outcomes of these wishes seemed crucial to me then. Now, when I am disappointed I realize that each disappointment opens other options for me. I did not believe that in high school because my wishes were more urgent then. But even now, it is difficult at times to feel relaxed about my wishes.

Sometimes attachments to things sneak up on me. I did not know how attached I was to my silver 1973 Volkswagen Superbeetle until it was stolen. Why would anyone steal my Beetle? There were so many better cars to choose from on our street. Soon after it was stolen, I began to realize how much I missed that little car. I recalled that I had had a VW Beetle since 1968. There was always a Beetle in the driveway. I taught my children to drive in Beetles. When they were little, they sat on my lap and learned to shift gears. There were a lot of memories associated with those cars, including bringing my younger son home from the hospital in one. I found myself looking for a replacement, but there aren't a lot of VWs in Milwaukee. The salt has eaten away at most of them.

Finally, I resigned myself to the fact that, at least for

now, I could live without a Beetle. I would still have the memories. After all, I ought to be able to practice what I preach: if you cannot imagine living without some possession, then the possession owns you instead of your owning it.

A few weeks later when I received a call from the police that they had found my Beetle pretty much unscathed, I was not entirely displeased. But I asked myself, "When did I learn to value a car so much?" Then I remembered Uncle Ted. He took great pride in his car, washing it, polishing it, and babying it just like a treasured person. Uncle Ted and Aunt Alma had no children. Aunt Alma had her dog and Uncle Ted had his car. Those were their children. I have real children and I will try to keep that distinction in mind when I overvalue things.

Attachment to being right is much harder to give up. When my children were young, I knew exactly how they should conduct themselves and exactly how and what they should strive for. Ah, what moments of pristine clarity! And oh, what an education I had coming to me. The humbling experiences of my childrearing education would fill a separate book. One moment that stands out in my memory was when I took my two sons and my two nieces fishing. With absolute confidence I showed them how to bait their hooks, how to cast from the pier into the ocean, and how to cast net for bait. It was not until hours later that I noticed that the children were catching all the fish and I was catching very few. I was happy to see them having so much fun but confused about the discrepancy in our success. Then my son told me that they were not fishing with my bait, but some they got from a man on the pier who seemed to be catching all the fish. They had switched bait without telling me because they did not want to hurt my feelings. They detected my attachment to being right. I suppose it was not hard to detect.

It was not long after that I burned the toast one morning. Cheerfully I suggested, "Oh, good, now we can fix it like they do at the Ritz." I scraped the toast with a knife until, in my eyes, it was the perfect golden brown. "There you go," I said proudly setting the toast in front of them. The children looked at each other and said in near unison, "Right, Dad." Until that moment I had not even considered the possibility that I was trying to fool the kids. I thought back to when I first heard the phrase, "just like they fix it at the Ritz." My grandfather Davison had burned the toast one morning when I was 8 or 9 years old. Cheerfully he suggested to me, "Oh, good, now we can fix it like they do at the Ritz." Until that moment, some thirty years later, it had not occurred to me that I had been duped. My children were my teachers.

Today I will try to recognize my attachment to outcomes, things, and my attachment to being right.

At the beginning and end of formal meditation repeat this exercise over several breath cycles: *Attachments are part of my story.*

Now, when you are ready, begin formal meditation.

Sit erect in your comfortable straight back chair with both feet planted on the floor. Put your hands on your legs or fold them in your lap. Breathe through your nose when you can. Close your eyes and notice your abdomen expand as you say "in" and contract as you say "out." Feel at peace as you follow your breath.

1. After meditation write this exercise on a card or piece of paper that you will look at several times today: *Attachments are part of my story.* Look at the exercise during the day and be still for a moment each time you do. When you are still, follow your breath, "in" and "out" as your abdomen rises and falls with your breath. Follow your breath through several cycles. Be at peace.

At the end of the day write in your journal one example of using this or any exercise to achieve a shift in perception that brought with it peace of mind. Remember your Disruptions Notebook.

2. At the end of formal meditation, try to think of some time during the day that you will be tempted to over-value some outcome, or some thing, or being right. Deal with the imagined situation with grace and good humor in your mind.

At the very end of the meditation see clearly in your mind the picture of your goal, in addition to peace of mind, for these eight weeks. Hold that picture. Notice the details. Feel at peace with that picture.

After meditation write this exercise on a card or piece of paper that you will look at several times today: *Attachments are part of my story*. Look at the exercise during the day and be still for a moment each time you do. When you are still, follow your breath, "in" and "out" as your abdomen rises and falls with your breath. Follow your breath through several cycles. Be at peace.

At the end of the day write in your journal one example of using this or any exercise to achieve a shift in perception that brought with it peace of mind. Remember your Disruptions Notebook.

3. At the end of formal meditation see if you can get in touch with some person or persons who taught you to be overly invested in outcomes, things, or being right.

Rebuke them and then let the bright light fill your heart and then your whole body. Let your warm bright light spread to them as you forgive them.

At the very end of the meditation see clearly in your mind the picture of your goal, in addition to peace of mind, for these eight weeks. Hold that picture. Notice the details. Feel at peace with that picture.

After meditation write this exercise on a card or piece of paper that you will look at several times today: *Attachments are part of my story*. Look at the exercise during the day and be still for a moment each time you do. When you are still, follow your breath, "in" and "out" as your abdomen rises and falls with your breath. Follow your breath through several cycles. Be at peace.

At the end of the day write in your journal one example of using this or any exercise to achieve a shift in perception that brought with it peace of mind. Remember your Disruptions Notebook.

EXERCISE 7

PEACE OF MIND IS MY ONLY GOAL.[42]

Letting go and seeking only peace is a good way to derive unexpected benefits. When I let peace of mind be my only goal, I am frequently surprised by the other good things that happen. Most of the time I use this lesson when I feel a sense of urgency about something or feel myself attached to some particular outcome. I ask myself, "What is my goal here?" "Do I want————, or do I want peace of mind?"

We had a big family Christmas this year. We were lucky enough to have my son's wife's parents and her sister and husband in our home over the Christmas holiday. Usually I would scurry about until the wee hours of the morning making arrangements for Christmas day and get myself frazzled in the process. This Christmas I asked myself, "Do I want a Christmas spectacular or do I want peace of mind?" I chose peace of mind and rather than having elaborate and clever gifts for everyone, we had a simple, traditional Christmas. We all helped prepare the turkey. We played bridge and watched football during the bridge game, mostly via instant replay. We took turns playing our favorite holiday music either on the piano, the guitar, or on my favorite instrument, the CD. It was a super holiday with plenty of time to visit with people I really enjoy. Our gifts were simple but appreciated.

One possible criticism of making peace of mind my only goal is that it may seem self-centered. Well, it is self-serving but not self-centered. Drs. Milton and Rose Friedman make an interesting point in their book *Free to Choose*:[43] they say that more good is done by people seek-

ing to better themselves than is done by people who aim
to help others, because by seeking to better ourselves we
must help others. Only a win-win policy will truly be re-
warded. In economic terms, only a market that rewards
all participants will survive. If I try to do good for others
without regard for myself I may be surprised to find an
even greater degree of self-interest kept from my awareness. Keeping my interest in mind must include rewards
for others. What are the skills that permit me to do this
optimally?

For me, the most important skill I have acquired in
experiencing peace of mind is to be able to sit with my
strong unpeaceful emotions and bodily sensations without judging them. If I can sit with fear, sadness, hate, lust,
guilt, shame, excitement and pain without judging these
feelings and above all without running from them I will
end up feeling peaceful. Strong feelings pass more quickly
if, like the ship in a storm, we turn the bow into the storm
rather than futilely attempting to outrun it. The knowledge I gained through my years of psychoanalysis has been
very useful in helping me sit with my feelings. But this
knowledge would not be useful if I did not spend some time
each day experiencing my emotions and bodily sensations
in meditation.

At the beginning and end of formal meditation read
this exercise and dedicate this day to seeking only peace
of mind.

Now, when you are ready, begin formal meditation.

Sit comfortably erect in your straight back chair with
both feet planted on the floor. Put your hands on your legs
or fold them in your lap. Breathe through your nose when
you can. Close your eyes and notice your abdomen expand

as you say "in" and contract as you say "out." Feel at peace as you follow your breath.

1. After meditation write this exercise on a card or piece of paper that you will look at several times today: *Peace of mind is my only goal.* Look at the exercise during the day and be still for a moment each time you do. When you are still, follow your breath, "in" and "out" as your abdomen rises and falls with your breath. Follow your breath through several cycles. Be at peace.

At the end of the day write in your journal one example of using this or any exercise to achieve a shift in perception that brought with it peace of mind. Remember your Disruptions Notebook.

2. In the last few minutes of formal meditation try to anticipate some situation in your life today that is likely to disrupt your peace of mind. Ask yourself, "Do I want——or do I want peace of mind?" Give peace of mind a try and see how things work out.

At the very end of the meditation see clearly in your mind the picture of your goal, in addition to peace of mind, for these eight weeks. Hold that picture. Notice the details. Feel at peace with that picture.

After meditation write this exercise on a card or piece of paper that you will look at several times today: *Peace of mind is my only goal.* Look at the exercise during the day and be still for a moment each time you do. When you are still, follow your breath, "in" and "out" as your abdomen rises and falls with your breath. Follow your breath through several cycles. Be at peace.

At the end of the day write in your journal one example of using this or any exercise to achieve a shift in perception that brought with it peace of mind. Remember your Disruptions Notebook.

3. In the last few minutes of formal meditation think about this lesson and remember someone in your life in the past who seemed to disrupt your peace of mind more frequently than others. Rebuke that person. Feel the strong negative feelings toward that person. When they pass let your bright light form in your heart and spread all over your body and finally to the other person in forgiveness. Feel peace of mind return.

At the very end of the meditation see clearly in your mind the picture of your goal, in addition to peace of mind, for these eight weeks. Hold that picture. Notice the details. Feel at peace with that picture.

After meditation write this exercise on a card or piece of paper that you will look at several times today: *Peace of mind is my only goal*. Look at the exercise during the day and be still for a moment each time you do. When you are still, follow your breath, "in" and "out" as your abdomen rises and falls with your breath. Follow your breath through several cycles. Be at peace.

At the end of the day write in your journal one example of using this or any exercise to achieve a shift in perception that brought with it peace of mind. Remember your Disruptions Notebook.

WEEK 4

Forgiveness Paves the Road to Peace.[44]

Forgiveness is mostly for myself. It spares me from carrying a burden of resentment; however, it does not mean that I condone the action I am forgiving. It does not mean that I might not oppose similar actions in the future. It means I choose to let go of angry thoughts and feelings associated with some perceived injustice, after I have fully experienced them, in order to restore peace of mind. Forgiveness is the opposite of carrying a grudge. It is healing for the forgiver.

In addition to reading the lessons, meditating, and journaling each day, remember to write in your Disruptions Notebook any major interruptions to your peace of mind this week. Remember that disruptions have two parts: (1) villains—people who are perceived as treating me poorly, and (2) fears—consequences I imagine occurring as a result of the villains' action. When I record a disruption, the more detail I include—about the characteristics of the villains and the imagined outcomes in my fears—the better.

As you move through the exercises, you may find that the example of healing that comes to mind at the end of the day is the implementation of an exercise other than the one you are studying. That is fine. The more familiar you are with the exercises, the more likely that is to happen. Write the moment of healing that comes to mind even if it does not have to do with the specific lesson you are studying. As you progress in your studies, you will see how all the lessons are connected.

EXERCISE 1

NOTHING CAN HURT ME BUT MY THOUGHTS AND FEELINGS.

Most of our problems come from reliving past problems by anticipating troubles that never happen. Even when the worst happens it is rarely as bad as we have imagined. I remember clearly a time when I took my two boys to a local fair. My older son, Mike, won a goldfish in a game. I felt compelled to help my younger son, Jeffrey, win a goldfish, too. We went home, put the fish in a bowl, and the boys talked to them off and on during the day. They named Mike's fish Ansel, and Jeff's fish Fred.

The next morning I was the first one up. I noticed Fred floating belly up in the fish bowl. Filled with fear that Jeff would react catastrophically to Fred's untimely demise, I rushed to a local pet store and bought an exact clone of Fred, rushed home, removed the dead fish, and placed the new Fred in the fish bowl. Mike and Jeff awakened, came downstairs, saw their fish, talked to them, and went outside to play. I wiped my brow, having narrowly averted a traumatic situation.

The next morning I awakened and went downstairs. Fred II was floating on the top of the water. The pet shop owner recognized me on sight. He ferreted out another Fred clone and I rushed home and made the switch mere moments before the boys came down for breakfast. They talked to the fish after breakfast and went out to play. What was happening here? Today, I would have recognized my sense of urgency as a clue that something was amiss, but at that time I was caught up in the drama as much as I could have been.

The next morning Fred III was floating on top of the water in the fish bowl. I heard the boys coming downstairs. Disaster was about to strike. My poor little son, Jeffrey, was about to be scarred for life. Luckily, he did not look at the fish bowl before breakfast. Maybe they would not notice after breakfast either and I could make another trip to the pet store. Alas, no such luck. On the way out to play Jeff went by the fish bowl and saw Fred floating there. He looked at me and said, "Look, Dad, Fred's dead." With that he turned and went outside to play. I scooped Fred out and did not replace him.

Years later, when Jeff was in junior high school reflecting on Fred's plight, Renée and I asked Jeff what he made of the bad luck with his gold fish. He answered, matter of factly, "Well, he probably died because when no one was around I took him out of the fish bowl and played with him. I didn't know then that would hurt him." The mystery of the "Freds" was solved and my worry about the trauma to my son was for naught.

Looking back on the situation I was reliving with my sons the difficulty my parents had talking with me about death. I was reliving the past in my actions with my sons. My fears of talking to my sons about death hurt me.

At the beginning and end of formal meditation repeat this exercise over several breath cycles: *Nothing can hurt me but my thoughts and feelings*.

Now, when you are ready, begin formal meditation.

Sit comfortably erect in your straight back chair with both feet planted on the floor. Put your hands on your legs or fold them in your lap. Breathe through your nose when you can. Close your eyes and notice your abdomen expand as you say "in" and contract as you say "out." Feel at peace as you follow your breath.

1. After meditation write this exercise on a card or piece of paper that you will look at several times today: *Nothing can hurt me but my thoughts and feelings.* Look at the exercise during the day and be still for a moment each time you do. When you are still, follow your breath, "in" and "out" as your abdomen rises and falls with your breath. Follow your breath through several cycles. Be at peace.

At the end of the day write in your journal one example of using this or any exercise to achieve a shift in perception that brought with it peace of mind. Remember your Disruptions Notebook.

2. In the last few minutes of formal meditation find a situation in your life today that you can imagine stimulating you to construct a catastrophic fantasy. Think of that catastrophic fantasy then remember the lesson for today.

At the very end of the meditation see clearly in your mind the picture of your goal, in addition to peace of mind, for these eight weeks. Hold that picture. Notice the details. Feel at peace with that picture.

After meditation write this exercise on a card or piece of paper that you will look at several times today: *Nothing can hurt me but my thoughts and feelings.* Look at the exercise during the day and be still for a moment each time you do. When you are still, follow your breath, "in" and "out" as your abdomen rises and falls with your breath. Follow your breath through several cycles. Be at peace.

At the end of the day write in your journal one example of using this or any exercise to achieve a shift in perception that brought with it peace of mind. Remember your Disruptions Notebook.

3. In the last few minutes of formal meditation remember a time in the past that you were stimulated to anticipate a catastrophic outcome. If someone else helped you catastrophize, think of that person and rebuke him. When your angry feelings have passed let the white light build within your heart; let the light fill and warm you. When you are ready, let that white light spread forgiveness to the person in your past who helped you believe in catastrophe.

At the very end of the meditation see clearly in your mind the picture of your goal, in addition to peace of mind, for these eight weeks. Hold that picture. Notice the details. Feel at peace with that picture.

After meditation write this exercise on a card or piece of paper that you will look at several times today: *Nothing can hurt me but my thoughts and feelings*. Look at the exercise during the day and be still for a moment each time you do.

At the end of the day write in your journal one example of using this or any exercise to achieve a shift in perception that brought with it peace of mind.

Exercise 2

I WILL FIND NO VALUE IN HOLDING ONTO BLAME.[45]

Blame is pointing the finger at someone in accusation. Blame has no value in its own right but it can be an important first step in healing. Through many years of psychoanalysis I learned to be freer to look critically at the adults who influenced me in my formative years. I remember complaining about my grandpa Davison who repeatedly planned fishing trips with me only to be detained by work at the last minute and unable to go. One day, years after completing psychoanalysis, I was telling a friend about our fishing planning sessions without a hint of acrimony. I was surprised how little I cared that Grandpa and I had never actually fished together. It was my grandmother who actually took me fishing to the river. And that was a pleasant memory in itself.

It did not seem to matter that my grandfather and I had not actualized our plan. I remember the hours we spent poring over the maps of the river, plotting where we were likely to find fish. The memories of our planning sessions took on a life of their own, and in my memory were devoid of the disappointment I had complained about years before in my psychoanalysis. It was then that I saw the link between my feeling free to look critically at my grandfather and retaining pleasant memories of our time together. Blame was the first step in healing those memories. So when I think of finding no value in blame, I mean no value other than as a first step in healing, not as an end in itself.

At the beginning and end of formal meditation repeat this exercises over several breath cycles: *I will find no value in holding onto blame.*

Now, when you are ready, begin formal meditation.

Sit comfortably erect in your straight back chair with both feet planted on the floor. Put your hands on your legs or fold them in your lap. Breathe through your nose when you can. Close your eyes and notice your abdomen expand as you say "in" and contract as you say "out." Feel at peace as you follow your breath.

1. After meditation write this exercise on a card or piece of paper that you will look at several times today: *I will find no value in holding onto blame.* Look at the exercise during the day and be still for a moment each time you do. When you are still, follow your breath, "in" and "out" as your abdomen rises and falls with your breath. Follow your breath through several cycles. Be at peace.

At the end of the day write in your journal one example of using this or any exercise to achieve a shift in perception that brought with it peace of mind. Remember your Disruptions Notebook.

2. In the last few minutes of formal meditation think of someone you may encounter today who is likely to stimulate blaming feelings in you. Imagine rebuking that person in your mind. When the critical, angry feelings have passed, forgive the person. Remember, you do not have to complete the forgiving process. All you have to do is acknowledge a willingness to forgive. The rest will take care of itself with the help of the force.

At the very end of the meditation see clearly in your

mind the picture of your goal, in addition to peace of mind, for these eight weeks. Hold that picture. Notice the details. Feel at peace with that picture.

After meditation write this exercise on a card or piece of paper that you will look at several times today: *I will find no value in holding onto blame*. Look at the exercise during the day and be still for a moment each time you do. When you are still, follow your breath, "in" and "out" as your abdomen rises and falls with your breath. Follow your breath through several cycles. Be at peace.

At the end of the day write in your journal one example of using this or any exercise to achieve a shift in perception that brought with it peace of mind. Remember your Disruptions Notebook.

3. In the last few minutes of formal meditation think back to someone in your past whom you have blamed for something. Feel the full force of that blame until the storm of feeling passes. When your angry feelings have subsided, let the white light build within your heart. Let it spread to fill and warm you. When you are ready, let that white light spread forgiveness to the person in the past who disappointed you. Let yourself and that person be warmed by your bright light of forgiveness, kindness, and compassion.

At the very end of the meditation see clearly in your mind the picture of your goal, in addition to peace of mind, for these eight weeks. Hold that picture. Notice the details. Feel at peace with that picture.

After meditation write this exercise on a card or piece of paper that you will look at several times today: *I will find no value in holding onto blame*. Look at the exercise during the day and be still for a moment each time you do. When you are still, follow your breath, "in" and "out" as your abdomen rises and falls with your breath. Follow your breath through several cycles. Be at peace.

At the end of the day write in your journal one example of using this or any exercise to achieve a shift in perception that brought with it peace of mind. Remember your Disruptions Notebook.

EXERCISE 3

I WILL FIND NO VALUE IN HOLDING ONTO GUILT.[46]

Guilt is blaming oneself. Guilt has value in two ways. It can be a useful signal that I am about to tread in dangerous territory, and it can show us where healing is needed.

As a signal, guilt sometimes brings some leftover, less than completely useful, remnants from childhood. These signals can be usefully updated in the light of our adult experience. The signal was created in childhood and at times may be worthless. Other times, though anachronistic, the hesitation a moment of guilt brings with it may be useful, indeed.

For example, I was about to cross the street in Washington between the Mall and the Lincoln Memorial when I noticed a tug from my conscience. The message was, "Do not cross the street without looking both ways or you will be in trouble with me." I remember learning this as a boy from my mother, my Aunt Betty, and my Grandma Kempf. So, as an adult I looked both ways. What made this an anachronistic rule for me as an adult is that this section of the Lincoln Memorial Circle is blocked from traffic by large yellow barricades that permit nothing to pass through. However, given the fact that crossing a street would rarely be so safe again, I might be better off to look both ways occasionally, when it is not necessary, rather than missing one occasion when it might be life saving. This signal of guilt that I was about to get in trouble with the mental image of my mother, aunt, and grandmother is not a bad one to keep around.

One message that is not so useful is "Do not begin a fight, but if the other guy hits you, let him have it." That was a rule my father taught me. It was not a bad rule for the first grade with a bully terrorizing my playground. Standing up to the bully was a good idea. It is not such a good rule now because it might, by extension, inspire me to strike back verbally when extending myself in love would be a more useful response.

The second use of guilt is as a beacon that lights a place where healing is needed. June, a cousin of mine, lost her mother to cancer when she was 12. June blamed herself, thinking that had she been a better daughter, with a purer heart, her mother would not have been taken from her. As a youngster and later as an adult she wept out of guilt and loss and seemed sad all the time.

Later in therapy and looking back on the situation, she was able to see how unfair her judgment had been. She was freed up to remember how her mother had inspired her artistic talents which she used to her advantage as an adult. Her mother was alive in her memories and in June's art. Giving up her harsh self-judgment allowed June to use those talents and abilities. In therapy June used her guilt to guide her to healing.

At the beginning and end of formal meditation bring this exercise to mind: *I will find no value in holding onto guilt*. Remember, guilt is sometimes a useful signal to find a place where correction might be made. It is not useful to hang on to guilt and to punish yourself indefinitely.

Now, when you are ready, begin formal meditation.

Sit comfortably erect in your straight back chair with both feet planted on the floor. Put your hands on your legs or fold them in your lap. Breathe through your nose when you can. Close your eyes and notice your abdomen expand as you say "in" and contract as you say "out." Feel at peace as you follow your breath.

1. After meditation write this exercise on a card or piece of paper that you will look at several times today: *I will find no value in holding onto guilt*. Look at the exercise during the day and be still for a moment each time you do. In that stillness, follow your breath, "in" and "out" as your abdomen rises and falls with your breath. Follow your breath through several cycles. Be at peace.

At the end of the day write in your journal one example of using this or any exercise to achieve a shift in perception that brought with it peace of mind. Remember your Disruptions Notebook.

2. In the last few minutes of formal meditation think of someone you may meet today who is likely to stimulate guilt in you. Imagine rebuking that person in your imagination and when the critical, angry feelings have passed, forgive her. Remember, you do not have to complete the forgiving process. All you have to do is acknowledge a willingness to forgive. The rest will take care of itself with the help of the force.

At the very end of the meditation see clearly in your mind the picture of your goal, in addition to peace of mind, for these eight weeks. Hold that picture. Notice the details. Feel at peace with that picture.

After meditation write this exercise on a card or piece of paper that you will look at several times today: *I will find no value in holding onto guilt*. Look at the exercise during the day and be still for a moment each time you do. When you are still, follow your breath, "in" and "out" as your abdomen rises and falls with your breath. Follow your breath through several cycles. Be at peace.

At the end of the day write in your journal one example of using this or any exercise to achieve a shift in perception that brought with it peace of mind. Remember your Disruptions Notebook.

3. At the end of formal meditation, think back to someone in your past who inspired guilt that was not useful for you. Feel the full force of rebuke against that person until the storm of feeling passes. When your angry feelings have passed let the white light build within your heart, fill you, and warm you. When you are ready, let that white light spread forgiveness to that person in your past who inspired irrational guilty feelings in you. Let yourself and that person be warmed by your bright light of forgiveness, kindness, and compassion.

At the very end of the meditation see clearly in your mind the picture of your goal, in addition to peace of mind, for these eight weeks. Hold that picture. Notice the details. Feel at peace with that picture.

After meditation write this exercise on a card or piece of paper that you will look at several times today: *I will find no value in holding onto guilt*. Look at the exercise during the day and be still for a moment each time you do. When you are still, follow your breath, "in" and "out" as your abdomen rises and falls with your breath. Follow your breath through several cycles. Be at peace.

At the end of the day write in your journal one example of using this or any exercise to achieve a shift in perception that brought with it peace of mind. Remember your Disruptions Notebook.

EXERCISE 4

MY FRIGHTENED-SELF SPEAKS FIRST.

I was recently at a meeting where one participant took issue with everything said by other committee members. He objected to the agenda. He objected to the format of the meeting. He objected to the wording of each proposal. I was tempted to become verbally strident. My frightened-self was screaming out for me to make a sarcastic comment. If I had followed that advice, we would have been mired in a debate about form and format and would never have addressed the substantive matters at hand.

Instead, I decided not to respond at all but to be quietly respectful of this person's opinions. I could not think of a way to respond verbally. I reminded myself that "my frightened-self speaks first" but "listening is love in action," so I listened. It worked out pretty well. After a while the objector calmed down and got busy helping us transact the business of our committee. This was a hard lesson for me to learn, for in our family the quick, clever, verbal rebuttal was valued.

I remember the character played by Albert Brooks in the movie, *Broadcast News*. His name was Aaron Altman and we first meet him as he gives the valedictory speech at his high school graduation. Since he is a prodigy he is graduating several years early. He says that his classmates had made his last few years a living hell and hopes they will be more sensitive the next time they meet someone like him, their mental superior. In the next scene we see the results of his provocations. Three ruffians are beating him while Aaron, true to form, is still trying to get in the last word. One might imagine that this beating could go on for some time, but the bullies tire physically before Aaron's tongue goes limp. As a parting shot Aaron screams, "These wounds will heal but here is something that will never go away . . . none of you will ever make more than $19,000 a year, you will never enjoy writing a well-turned phrase . . . and you will never leave south Boston, while I will see the whole damn world!" The ruffians walk away, but one turns to the other and says, "Hey, $19,000 a year . . . not bad!" A title emerges under Aaron's image: "Future Network News Correspondent."

Aaron's insensitivity to others is hard to overstate. One might speculate that he comes from a background where getting in the last word is valued even more than it was in my family. One might also speculate that Aaron is not expecting retaliation for smart remarks. Poor Aaron. Despite all his intelligence and talent, this trend toward miscalculation of interpersonal consequences ruins his chance to become a network anchor. He cannot learn that some sensitive people never forgive a smart remark about their receding hair lines. He misses no opportunity to use his intelligence, mostly with men, in ways that do not endear him. When he gets his big chance to anchor the weekend news he is so sure everyone will hate him that he develops a bad case of the "flop sweats," that is, sweating so profusely that he looks like he might flop over at any moment. He appears pitiful to the brass. Finally, he sees the handwriting on the wall and takes a local anchor job in a smaller market, a part of the "whole damn world" his earlier prediction did not fully anticipate. His frightened-self caused him a world of hurt.

At the beginning and end of formal meditation repeat this exercise over several breath cycles: *My frightened-self speaks first.* Make a resolution to let your first reaction go unsaid when it comes from your frightened-self. Be aware of it, but do not act on it.

Now, when you are ready, begin formal meditation.

Sit comfortably erect in your straight back chair with both feet planted on the floor. Put your hands on your legs or fold them in your lap. Breathe through your nose when you can. Close your eyes and notice your abdomen expand as you say "in" and contract as you say "out." Feel at peace as you follow your breath.

1. After meditation write this exercise on a card or piece of paper that you will look at several times today: *My frightened-self speaks first.* Look at the exercise during the day and be still for a moment each time you do. When you are still, follow your breath, "in" and "out" as your abdomen rises and falls with your breath. Follow your breath through several cycles. Be at peace.

At the end of the day write in your journal one example of using this or any exercise to achieve a shift in perception that brought with it peace of mind. Remember your Disruptions Notebook.

2. In the last few minutes of formal meditation think of someone you will encounter today who is likely to stimulate a smart remark from you. Imagine rebuking that person in your imagination and when the critical, angry feelings have passed, forgive the person. Remember, you do not have to complete the forgiving process. All you have to do is acknowledge a willingness to forgive. The rest will take care of itself with the help of the force.

At the very end of the meditation see clearly in your mind the picture of your goal, in addition to peace of mind, for these eight weeks. Hold that picture. Notice the details. Feel at peace with that picture.

After meditation write this exercise on a card or piece of paper that you will look at several times today: *My frightened-self speaks first*. Look at the exercise during the day and be still for a moment each time you do. When you are still, follow your breath, "in" and "out" as your abdomen rises and falls with your breath. Follow your breath through several cycles. Be at peace.

At the end of the day write in your journal one example of using this or any exercise to achieve a shift in perception that brought with it peace of mind. Remember your Disruptions Notebook.

3. In the last few minutes of formal meditation think back to a time in your past when you reacted from your frightened-self. Feel the full force of your feelings concerning that situation. If you feel guilty, feel the guilt until it passes, then remember that guilt is useful as a beacon to heal. Forgive yourself. When your guilty feelings have passed, let the white light build within you, fill you, and warm you. When you are ready, let that white light spread forgiveness to that person in your past who encouraged you to react rather than respond. Let yourself and that person be warmed by your bright light of forgiveness, kindness, and compassion.

At the very end of the meditation see clearly in your mind the picture of your goal, in addition to peace of mind, for these eight weeks. Hold that picture. Notice the details. Feel at peace with that picture.

After meditation write this exercise on a card or piece of paper that you will look at several times today: *My frightened-self speaks first*. Look at the exercise during the day and be still for a moment each time you do. When you are still, follow your breath, "in" and "out" as your abdomen rises and falls with your breath. Follow your breath through several cycles. Be at peace.

At the end of the day write in your journal one example of using this or any exercise to achieve a shift in perception that brought with it peace of mind. Remember your Disruptions Notebook.

**COMPARISON DISRUPTS
MY PEACE OF MIND.**

Comparison as it is used here means quietly competing in my own mind. Few mental activities are so surely disruptive to peace of mind as constantly comparing myself with someone else. It is equally disruptive if I see myself as the winner or as loser in the comparison. Comparison is the opposite of experiencing our connection and experiencing the blessing of this precious moment. So an antidote to comparison is to return my attention to this moment, my breath, and the perfection of this precious moment. Or I might shift my focus to similarities rather than differences.

No one makes a case for being in the moment any better than Thich Nhat Hanh. In the book, *The Miracle of Mindfulness,* he reminds us that "one should not lose oneself in mind dispersion or in one's surroundings (p. 22)."[47] I think that to Thich Nhat Hanh, comparison would be mind dispersion. Not only is comparison pretty useless, but our assessments are so often wrong.

I remember one student to whom I felt vastly superior during a significant part of our medical school education. I made better grades than he did; I belonged to a fraternity and he did not. I had a motor scooter and he didn't. In how many other ways could a person be superior?

Then one day I learned that he had volunteered his time to helping the poor, while I was busy leading the good life. Oops! I learned that he provided medical assistance to the inhabitants of island neighborhoods in the Charleston area where there was no medical care. Oops! I learned

that he worked in a factory during his breaks from school
to pay for his education. Oops! My estimation for him grew,
and my comparisons proved as groundless as any comparison could be.

On the other end of the range of comparisons, I remember one of my first birthday parties. One of my friends
came dressed in a sailor's uniform. I was so envious I could
not take my eyes off him! I was green with envy. Everything about the birthday party made me miserable. All the
pictures of that birthday party show me leering enviously
at the boy in the sailor's suit.

Analyzing these two different experiences convinced
me that they were connected. I hated to feel envy. I imagined as a little boy that having a sailor suit would make
me a warrior, as big as my father who wore a Navy uniform when he was on leave from war. Later in life, in order
to avoid envy, I often focused my attention on someone I
felt superior to.

I began to discount comparison when I learned that
people tend to undervalue what is easy for them. If it is
easy then it must not be worth much. I have known tal-
ented musicians who simply did not value their talent
because playing was so easy for them. The same goes for
writers, artists, and sculptors. We need to honor what
we do easily because it may be a sign of our talents. The
better we are acquainted with our talents, the better we
know where to invest our energy to reap the greatest
satisfaction.

At the beginning and end of formal meditation repeat
this exercise over several breath cycles: *Comparison disrupts my peace of mind.*

Now, when you are ready, begin formal meditation.
Sit comfortably erect in your straight back chair with

both feet planted on the floor. Put your hands on your legs or fold them in your lap. Breathe through your nose when you can. Close your eyes and notice your abdomen expand as you say "in" and contract as you say "out." Feel at peace as you follow your breath.

1. After meditation write this exercise on a card or piece of paper that you will look at several times today: *Comparison disrupts my peace of mind.* Look at the exercise during the day and be still for a moment each time you do. When you are still, follow your breath, "in" and "out" as your abdomen rises and falls with your breath. Follow your breath through several cycles. Be at peace.

At the end of the day write in your journal one example of using this or any exercise to achieve a shift in perception that brought with it peace of mind. Remember your Disruptions Notebook.

2. In the last few minutes of formal meditation think of someone you will encounter today who is likely to stimulate your comparing yourself to her. Imagine seeing that person and feeling like her rather than separate.

At the very end of the meditation see clearly in your mind the picture of your goal, in addition to peace of mind, for these eight weeks. Hold that picture. Notice the details. Feel at peace with that picture.

After meditation write this exercise on a card or piece of paper that you will look at several times today: *Comparison disrupts my peace of mind.* Look at the exercise during the day and be still for a moment each time you do. When you are still, follow your breath, "in" and "out" as your abdomen rises and falls with your breath. Follow your breath through several cycles. Be at peace.

At the end of the day write in your journal one example of using this or any exercise to achieve a shift in perception that brought with it peace of mind. Remember your Disruptions Notebook.

3. In the last few minutes of formal meditation think back to a time in your past when you learned to compare yourself with others. Remember a person who taught you to compare. Feel the full force of your feelings concerning that situation. If you feel angry, feel the anger. If you feel guilty, feel the guilt. When your feelings are quiet let the white light build within your heart. Then let it fill you, and warm you. When you are ready let that white light spread forgiveness to that person in the past who taught you to compare rather than find similarities. Let yourself and that person be warmed by your bright light of forgiveness, kindness, and compassion.

At the very end of the meditation see clearly in your mind the picture of your goal, in addition to peace of mind, for these eight weeks. Hold that picture. Notice the details. Feel at peace with that picture.

After meditation write this exercise on a card or piece of paper that you will look at several times today: *Comparison disrupts my peace of mind.* Look at the exercise during the day and be still for a moment each time you do. When you are still, follow your breath, "in" and "out" as your abdomen rises and falls with your breath. Follow your breath through several cycles. Be at peace.

At the end of the day write in your journal one example of using this or any exercise to achieve a shift in perception that brought with it peace of mind. Remember your Disruptions Notebook.

EXERCISE 6

SEEING SIMILARITY IS A
KEY TO FORGIVENESS.

As long as we see ourselves as superior or inferior to others it is not so easy to see ourselves as similar. Recognizing that we are all similar and there is no action that anyone has committed that I have not committed (at least in my mind) is a key to forgiveness. At-one-ment means we are all part of a singular organism in the life force. What injury I do to you, I do to myself.

I learned this lesson the hard way in my youth. I was afraid to fight so I fought frequently. I even became a boxer. When I won, I usually had hurt my hands. When I lost, I usually had been hurt in other places as well, but win or lose, I hurt and so did my opponent. It is far less painful to recognize the truth. We are one. You have not done anything that I have not done at least once in my imagination. With that in mind, forgiveness is easy.

At the beginning and end of formal meditation repeat this exercise over several breath cycles: *Seeing similarity is a key to forgiveness.*

Now, when you are ready, begin formal meditation.

Sit comfortably erect in your straight back chair with both feet planted on the floor. Put your hands on your legs or fold them in your lap. Breathe through your nose when you can. Close your eyes and notice your abdomen expand as you say "in" and contract as you say "out." Feel at peace as you follow your breath.

1. After meditation write this exercise on a card or piece of paper that you will look at several times today: *Seeing similarity is a key to forgiveness.* Look at the exercise during the day and be still for a moment each time you do. When you are still, follow your breath, "in" and "out" as your abdomen rises and falls with your breath. Follow your breath through several cycles. Be at peace.

At the end of the day write in your journal one example of using this or any exercise to achieve a shift in perception that brought with it peace of mind. Remember your Disruptions Notebook.

2. In the last few minutes of formal meditation think of someone today whom you are likely to experience as separate from you. Let yourself feel separate, feel blame or any other separating emotion until the feelings become quiet, then look at the two of you in a different dimension. See yourself exchanging atoms and information with that other person. If that person has injured you, remember that he was injured, too. Forgive him. As the Eagles say in their song, "*Get over it.*"

At the very end of the meditation see clearly in your mind the picture of your goal, in addition to peace of mind, for these eight weeks. Hold that picture. Notice the details. Feel at peace with that picture.

After meditation write this exercise on a card or piece of paper that you will look at several times today: *Seeing similarity is a key to forgiveness.* Look at the exercise during the day and be still for a moment each time you do. When you are still, follow your breath, "in" and "out" as your abdomen rises and falls with your breath. Follow your breath through several cycles. Be at peace.

At the end of the day write in your journal one example of using this or any exercise to achieve a shift in per-

ception that brought with it peace of mind. Remember your Disruptions Notebook.

3. In the last few minutes of formal meditation think back to a time in your past when you learned to see yourself as separate from others. Remember a person who taught you to see yourself that way. Feel the full force of your feelings concerning that person. If you feel angry, feel the anger. If you feel guilty, feel the guilt. When your feelings are quiet, let the white light build within your heart. Then let it fill you, and warm you. When you are ready let the white light spread forgiveness to that person in the past who taught you to see differences rather than similarities. Allow yourself and that person to be warmed by your bright light of forgiveness, kindness, and compassion.

At the very end of the meditation see clearly in your mind the picture of your goal, in addition to peace of mind, for these eight weeks. Hold that picture. Notice the details. Feel at peace with that picture.

After meditation write this exercise on a card or piece of paper that you will look at several times today: *Seeing similarity is a key to forgiveness*. Look at the exercise during the day and be still for a moment each time you do. When you are still, follow your breath, "in" and "out" as your abdomen rises and falls with your breath. Follow your breath through several cycles. Be at peace.

At the end of the day write in your journal one example of using this or any exercise to achieve a shift in perception that brought with it peace of mind. Remember your Disruptions Notebook.

I HAVE A CHOICE TO SEE
PEACE OR CONFLICT.[48]

What I see outside myself is dependent on what I feel inside myself. A rowdy, irritating, mean, bratty child becomes a poor, frightened little boy as soon as we learn that his mother just died. If I have so much control over what I see then there is no reason why I should feel upset for any length of time. Once I learn to follow my breath, peace is just a breath away. The power of breath is illustrated in a story by Thich Nhat Hanh in his book *The Miracle of Mindfulness* about a tall tower. From its top a person can see for very long distances. The tower, however, has no ladder to climb it. There is only a thread that passes from the ground over the top of the tower to the ground on the other side. A thoughtful person might attach a string to one end of the thread and pull the other end until the string went over the tower. Then he might attach a rope to the string and pull it over the tower until it reaches the ground. By attaching the rope to an immovable object, a rope ladder could be installed that would permit a person to climb to the top of the tower. Our breath is such a thread, delicate but with great potential power for achieving peace of mind when we learn to use it properly. To use our breath properly we can return to it at moments through out the day. We can notice it and recognize that when we think of our breath we have everything we need.

Our daily lives can become so full of hustle and bustle that we forget: *I have a choice to see peace or conflict.* Whenever I begin to get caught up with my "To Do List," I try to remember to invoke this exercise.

At the beginning and end of formal meditation repeat this lesson over several breath cycles: *I have a choice to see peace or conflict.*

Now, when you are ready, begin formal meditation.

Sit comfortably erect in your straight back chair with both feet planted on the floor. Put your hands on your legs or fold them in your lap. Breathe through your nose when you can. Close your eyes and notice your abdomen expand as you say "in" and contract as you say "out." Feel at peace as you follow your breath.

1. After meditation write this exercise on a card or piece of paper that you will look at several times today: *I have a choice to see peace or conflict.* Look at the exercise during the day and be still for a moment each time you do. When you are still, follow your breath, "in" and "out" as your abdomen rises and falls with your breath. Follow your breath through several cycles. Be at peace.

At the end of the day write in your journal one example of using this or any exercise to achieve a shift in perception that brought with it peace of mind. Remember your Disruptions Notebook.

2. In the last few minutes of formal meditation think of someone today whom you are likely to experience as disrupting your peace of mind. Imagine the feelings accompanying that situation. Then remember the lesson: I could see peace instead of this. Turn your attention to your breath. Remember the tower. Feel peace as you follow your breath.

At the very end of the meditation see clearly in your mind the picture of your goal, in addition to peace of mind,

for these eight weeks. Hold that picture. Notice the details. Feel at peace with that picture.

After meditation write this exercise on a card or piece of paper that you will look at several times today: *I have a choice to see peace or conflict*. Look at the exercise during the day and be still for a moment each time you do. When you are still, follow your breath, "in" and "out" as your abdomen rises and falls with your breath. Follow your breath through several cycles. Be at peace.

At the end of the day write in your journal one example of using this or any exercise to achieve a shift in perception that brought with it peace of mind. Remember your Disruptions Notebook.

3. In the last few minutes of formal meditation think back to a time in your past to someone who disrupted your peace of mind. Feel the full force of your feelings toward that person. If you feel angry, feel the anger. If you feel guilty, feel the guilt. When your feelings are quiet, let the white light build within your heart. Then let it fill you, and warm you. When you are ready, let that white light spread forgiveness to the person who disrupted your peace of mind. Let yourself and that person be warmed by your bright light of forgiveness, kindness, and compassion.

At the very end of the meditation see clearly in your mind the picture of your goal, in addition to peace of mind, for these eight weeks. Hold that picture. Notice the details. Feel at peace with that picture.

After meditation write this exercise on a card or piece of paper that you will look at several times today: *I have a choice to see peace or conflict*. Look at the exercise during the day and be still for a moment each time you do.

When you are still, follow your breath, "in" and "out" as your abdomen rises and falls with your breath. Follow your breath through several cycles. Be at peace.

At the end of the day write in your journal one example of using this or any exercise to achieve a shift in perception that brought with it peace of mind. Remember your Disruptions Notebook.

WEEK 5

Healing Is My
Choice to Make[49]

I can heal anytime I wish merely by focusing on my breath. Once I am certain that I can do this, I have power of significant proportions that I can use for myself and all those around me. One of my colleagues, Steve Steury, is known for the calming influence he has on the most strident opposition in meetings. He simply calms himself, and everyone else in the meeting seems to calm down with him. He speaks slowly in a conciliatory way. He emphasizes similarities rather than differences, and it has a hypnotic influence on those around him. In order to be able to do this, he first learned to heal himself.

In addition to reading the exercises, meditating and journaling each day, remember to write

in your Disruptions Notebook any major interruptions to your peace of mind this week. Be
attentive to the personality characteristics of
those who play a part in your disruptions. Write
down those characteristics in as much detail as
possible. Also write down the details of your
fears in your Disruptions Notebook.

EXERCISE 1

HEALING IS A SHIFT IN PERCEPTION THAT BRINGS ME PEACE OF MIND.[50]

Once, when I was about 7, my Uncle Ted and I went to the store to buy groceries. The man who helped us put the groceries in the trunk of Uncle Ted's car picked me up, threw me into the air and caught me. I was frightened. Uncle Ted took me from the man and put me in the car. Later he told me that he had not said anything to him because he was not sure how stable the guy was. At the time, although I did not say anything to Uncle Ted, I was angry at him for not being more forceful in my defense. Remember, I was operating under the rule that I had learned at 6, "If the other guy does something wrong first, then you can slug him." At the time I was looking for reasons to slug guys, having been primed by an earlier victory over a playground bully.

In meditation I remembered this incident. I can see now how wise Uncle Ted had been. Where I once labeled him "chicken," I now see him as wise. I feel at peace over this memory because the shift in perception healed an old wound. I can let my bright, white light fill both of us in a moment of healing.

At the beginning and end of formal meditation repeat this exercise over several breath cycles: *Healing is a shift in perception that brings me peace of mind.*

Now, when you are ready, begin formal meditation.

Sit comfortably erect in your straight back chair with both feet planted on the floor. Put your hands on your legs or fold them in your lap. Breathe through your nose when you can. Close your eyes and notice your abdomen expand

as you say "in" and contract as you say "out." Feel at peace as you follow your breath.

1. After meditation write this exercise on a card or piece of paper that you will look at several times today: *Healing is a shift in perception that brings me peace of mind*. Look at the exercise during the day and be still for a moment each time you do. When you are still, follow your breath, "in" and "out" as your abdomen rises and falls with your breath. Follow your breath through several cycles. Be at peace.

At the end of the day write in your journal one example of using this or any exercise to achieve a shift in perception that brought with it peace of mind. Remember the Disruptions Notebook.

2. In the last few minutes of formal meditation think of someone you may meet today who is likely to disrupt your peace of mind. Imagine the encounter and imagine your being attentive and undefensive with this person. Imagine your genuine attentiveness changing the encounter.

At the very end of the meditation see clearly in your mind the picture of your goal, in addition to peace of mind, for these eight weeks. Hold that picture. Notice the details. Feel at peace with that picture.

After meditation write this exercise on a card or piece of paper that you will look at several times today: *Healing is a shift in perception that brings me peace of mind*. Look at the exercise during the day and be still for a moment each time you do. When you are still, follow your breath, "in" and "out" as your abdomen rises and falls with your breath. Follow your breath through several cycles. Be at peace.

At the end of the day write in your journal one example of using this or any exercise to achieve a shift in perception that brought with it peace of mind. Remember your Disruptions Notebook.

3. In the last few minutes of formal meditation think back to a time in your past to someone who disrupted your peace of mind. Feel the full force of your feelings toward that person. When your feelings are quiet, let the white light build within your heart. Then let it fill you and warm you. When you are ready, let that white light spread forgiveness to that person in the past who disrupted your peace of mind. Let yourself and that person be warmed by your bright light of forgiveness, kindness, and compassion.

At the very end of the meditation see clearly in your mind the picture of your goal, in addition to peace of mind, for these eight weeks. Hold that picture. Notice the details. Feel at peace with that picture.

After meditation write this exercise on a card or piece of paper that you will look at several times today: *Healing is a shift in perception that brings me peace of mind.* Look at the exercise during the day and be still for a moment each time you do. When you are still, follow your breath, "in" and "out" as your abdomen rises and falls with your breath. Follow your breath through several cycles. Be at peace.

At the end of the day write in your journal one example of using this or any exercise to achieve a shift in perception that brought with it peace of mind. Remember your Disruptions Notebook.

HEALING ACCOMPANIES MY SEEING SOMEONE ANGRY AS ONE WHO IS FRIGHTENED AND CALLING OUT FOR HELP.[51]

The day before a birthday party Renée and I were hosting for my good friend, Gholi, I acted like an angry bear. I stomped and fumed about the preparations. I was making a masochist's delight of what should have been fun. I hated the seating arrangement and the wine tasted bitter. The chairs were too close, and the tablecloths did not match. Also, the plates were too white!

Renée asked, "What's frightening you?" Immediately I calmed down because I could see that was right. In my meditation that day I remembered my early experience with birthday parties and especially being miserable when my friend wore his sailor suit. I was afraid I was going to experience a party as miserable as that one had been. But times are different, and I now have a choice about how I experience things.

Renée reached out in love to me rather than stooping to my level of irritability. It made all the difference. Moreover, we had a great birthday party. It was so great that Gholi wrote, saying that his cousin had just confirmed that we were off one year on his age. So we would have to recelebrate the same birthday the same way next year.

At the beginning and end of formal meditation repeat this exercise over several breath cycles: *Healing accompanies my seeing someone angry as one who is frightened and calling out for help.*

Now, when you are ready, begin formal meditation. Sit comfortably erect in your straight back chair with both feet planted on the floor. Put your hands on your legs or fold them in your lap. Breathe through your nose when you can. Close your eyes and notice your abdomen expand as you say "in" and contract as you say "out." Feel at peace as you follow your breath.

1. After meditation write this exercise on a card or piece of paper that you will look at several times today: *Healing accompanies my seeing someone angry as one who is frightened and calling out for help.* Look at the lesson during the day and be still for a moment each time you do. When you are still, follow your breath, "in" and "out" as your abdomen rises and falls with your breath. Follow your breath through several cycles. Be at peace.

At the end of the day write in your journal one example of using this or any exercise to achieve a shift in perception that brought with it peace of mind. Remember your Disruptions Notebook.

2. In the last few minutes of formal meditation think of someone you may meet today who is likely to disrupt your peace of mind. Imagine an encounter with that person. Imagine that person being disruptive, and that you recognize this as fear. Your recognition allows you to be attentive to and not defensive with this person. Imagine genuine attentiveness as a reaching out in love to a frightened person.

At the very end of the meditation see clearly in your mind the picture of your goal, in addition to peace of mind, for these eight weeks. Hold that picture. Notice the details. Feel at peace with that picture.

After meditation write this exercise on a card or piece of paper that you will look at several times today: *Heal-*

ing accompanies my seeing someone angry as one who is frightened and calling out for help. Look at the exercise during the day and be still for a moment each time you do. When you are still, follow your breath, "in" and "out" as your abdomen rises and falls with your breath. Follow your breath through several cycles. Be at peace.

At the end of the day write in your journal one example of using this or any exercise to achieve a shift in perception that brought with it peace of mind. Remember your Disruptions Notebook.

3. In the last few minutes of formal meditation think back to a time in your past to someone who acted angrily toward you. Feel the full force of your feelings toward that person. When your feelings are quiet, remind yourself that the other person was frightened. Notice how that recognition changes the way you see things.

When you are ready, let the white light build within your heart. Then let it fill you and warm you. After a few moments let that white light spread forgiveness to that person in the past who disrupted your peace of mind. Let yourself and that person be warmed by your bright light of forgiveness, kindness, and compassion.

At the very end of the meditation see clearly in your mind the picture of your goal, in addition to peace of mind, for these eight weeks. Hold that picture. Notice the details. Feel at peace with that picture.

After meditation write this exercise on a card or piece of paper that you will look at several times today: *Healing accompanies my seeing someone angry as one who is frightened and calling out for help*. Look at the exercise during the day and be still for a moment each time you do. When you are still, follow your breath, "in" and "out" as your abdomen rises and falls with your breath. Follow your breath through several cycles. Be at peace.

At the end of the day write in your journal one example of using this or any exercise to achieve a shift in perception that brought with it peace of mind. Remember your Disruptions Notebook.

EXERCISE 3

HEALING OCCURS WHEN I RECOGNIZE MY IRRITABILITY AS FEAR.[52]

After a recent break for the holidays I looked at my schedule and it seemed much too full. I felt my friend, "the bear" (my frightened-self) come out as I barked orders to my office helpers. Sue, my office manager, raised her eyebrows and gave me her "over the glasses" scowl. That was a sign that I had gone too far. I looked within myself and could see that my frightened-self, the bear, was taking over. In my meditation I remembered a time in my life after my encounter with the model airplane that I could not put together. For a period of time, when I awakened in the morning, I feared that I wouldn't be able to do anything satisfying that day. I rushed around like a long-tailed cat in a room full of rocking chairs, afraid that anything I might encounter would expose my littleness and my vulnerability. So, the sight of my packed schedule evoked a similar response in me. But unlike that earlier situation, I could help myself; I developed a plan. I asked Sue to rearrange a few meetings, and the problem was solved.

At the beginning and end of formal meditation repeat this exercise over several breath cycles: *Healing occurs when I recognize my irritability as fear.*

Now, when you are ready, begin formal meditation.

Sit comfortably erect in your straight back chair with both feet planted on the floor. Put your hands on your legs or fold them in your lap. Breathe through your nose when you can. Close your eyes and notice your abdomen expand as you say "in" and contract as you say "out." Feel at peace as you follow your breath.

1. After meditation write this exercise on a card or piece of paper that you will look at several times today: *Healing occurs when I recognize my irritability as fear.* Look at the exercise during the day and be still for a moment each time you do. When you are still, follow your breath, "in" and "out" as your abdomen rises and falls with your breath. Follow your breath through several cycles. Be at peace.

At the end of the day write in your journal one example of using this or any exercise to achieve a shift in perception that brought with it peace of mind. Remember your Disruptions Notebook.

2. In the last few minutes of formal meditation think of something you will encounter today that is likely to evoke irritability in you. Imagine that occurrence and feeling irritable. Imagine recognizing this irritability as fear. Imagine calming yourself, turning to your breath, and feeling peace. Later you may look into your past and figure out where that fearfulness comes from.

At the very end of the meditation see clearly in your mind the picture of your goal, in addition to peace of mind, for these eight weeks. Hold that picture. Notice the details. Feel at peace with that picture.

After meditation write this exercise on a card or piece of paper that you will look at several times today: *Healing occurs when I recognize my irritability as fear.* Look at the exercise during the day and be still for a moment each time you do. When you are still, follow your breath, "in" and "out" as your abdomen rises and falls with your breath. Follow your breath through several cycles. Be at peace.

At the end of the day write in your journal one example of using this or any exercise to achieve a shift in per-

ception that brought with it peace of mind. Remember
your Disruptions Notebook.

3. In the last few minutes of formal meditation think
back to a time in your past when your "bear" came out.
Feel the full force of your irritable, frightened feelings.
When your feelings are quiet, remind yourself that you
were in error then. You were frightened when you acted
irritably. See if you can identify what was frightening you.
Notice how that recognition changes the way you see
things.

When you are ready, let the white light build within
your heart, fill you and warm you. Forgive yourself. Let
yourself be warmed by your bright light of forgiveness,
kindness, and compassion. Let the bright light spill over
to the other person and feel peace.

At the very end of the meditation see clearly in your
mind the picture of your goal, in addition to peace of mind,
for these eight weeks. Hold that picture. Notice the details. Feel at peace with that picture.

After meditation write this exercise on a card or piece
of paper that you will look at several times today: *Healing occurs when I recognize my irritability as fear*. Look
at the exercise during the day and be still for a moment
each time you do. When you are still, follow your breath,
"in" and "out" as your abdomen rises and falls. Follow your
breath through several cycles. Be at peace.

At the end of the day write in your journal one example of using this or any exercise to achieve a shift in perception that brought with it peace of mind. Remember
your Disruptions Notebook.

EXERCISE 4

HEALING IS OF THE MOMENT.[53]

This precious moment is all the time there is. The past is gone and the future is not yet here. If I live in the moment, I live in peace. This moment is a gift. That is why we call it the present. Anytime during the day that I pause for a moment and let myself experience my breath over three breath cycles, I feel peace. This is independent of outside circumstances.

Recently I went to the dentist—never one of my favorite activities. I tend to see anyone with a D.D.S. as a close relative of the dentist in the film *Little Shop of Horrors,* but less compassionate. During a moment while my dentist was drilling out an old filling, I turned my attention to my breath. Peace of mind returned immediately. That was as impressive a lesson as I could teach myself.

During my meditation that evening I recalled my experiences from childhood that made me so afraid of dentists. When I was still a preschooler, I had some cavities in my baby teeth. I was taken to the dentist who insisted that my parents leave the room as he drilled my teeth without anesthesia. After a few moments of drilling I was afraid to be alone with him, and the pain to my undeveloped nervous system seemed excruciating.

It is important to remember that today I do not need to feel abandoned in the dentist's chair. The force is always with me. And since we have local anesthesia now, I do not need to feel excruciating pain. No one is more interested in keeping the experience as pain free as possible than my dentist.

At the beginning and end of formal meditation repeat this exercise over several breath cycles: *Healing is of the moment.*

Now, when you are ready, begin formal meditation.

Sit comfortably erect in your straight back chair with both feet planted on the floor. Put your hands on your legs or fold them in your lap. Breathe through your nose when you can. Close your eyes and notice your abdomen expand as you say "in" and contract as you say "out." Feel at peace as you follow your breath.

1. After meditation write this exercise on a card or piece of paper that you will look at several times today: *Healing is of the moment.* Look at the exercise during the day and be still for a moment each time you do. When you are still, follow your breath, "in" and "out" as your abdomen rises and falls with your breath. Follow your breath through several cycles. Be at peace.

At the end of the day write in your journal one example of using this or any exercise to achieve a shift in perception that brought with it peace of mind. Remember your Disruptions Notebook.

2. In the last few minutes of formal meditation think of something you will encounter today that is likely to evoke tension in you. Imagine that occurrence. Imagine feeling tense and recognize this tension as fear. Imagine calming yourself, turning to your breath, and feeling peace. Later you may look into your past and figure out where that fearfulness came from.

At the very end of the meditation see clearly in your mind the picture of your goal, in addition to peace of mind,

for these eight weeks. Hold that picture. Notice the details. Feel at peace with that picture.

After meditation write this exercise on a card or piece of paper that you will look at several times today: *Healing is of the moment*. Look at the exercise during the day and be still for a moment each time you do. When you are still, follow your breath, "in" and "out" as your abdomen rises and falls with your breath. Follow your breath through several cycles. Be at peace.

At the end of the day write in your journal one example of using this or any exercise to achieve a shift in perception that brought with it peace of mind. Remember your Disruptions Notebook.

3. In the last few minutes of formal meditation think back to a time in your past when you were very tense. Feel the full force of that tension. When your feelings are quiet, remind yourself that in the past you did not have the option of turning to your breath. Try to identify what was frightening you then. Notice how that recognition changes the way you see things. Turn to your breath.

When you are ready, let the white light build within your heart. Let it fill you, and warm you. Calm yourself. Let yourself be warmed by your bright light of forgiveness, kindness, and compassion. Then, when you are ready, let your warm bright light flow to another person to be healed with you.

At the very end of the meditation see clearly in your mind the picture of your goal, in addition to peace of mind, for these eight weeks. Hold that picture. Notice the details. Feel at peace with that picture.

After meditation write this exercise on a card or piece

of paper that you will look at several times today: *Healing is of the moment*. Look at the exercise during the day and be still for a moment each time you do. When you are still, follow your breath, "in" and "out" as your abdomen rises and falls with your breath. Follow your breath through several cycles. Be at peace.

At the end of the day write in your journal one example of using this or any exercise to achieve a shift in perception that brought with it peace of mind. Remember your Disruptions Notebook.

HEALING IS TAKING PLEASURE IN ORDINARY ACTIVITIES.

One way to shift perception from worry to peace of mind is to focus on the pleasure of the moment. No matter what I am doing—typing, raking, making coffee, listening, or hugging my poodles—if I focus on the pleasure in my ordinary activities, I feel peace of mind. If I make a ritual out of ordinary activities, I feel peace.

Poodle-hugging is one of my favorite activities. My poodles and I have a regular ritual. When I come home from the office, they are usually in the "barkatorium," guarding the house from intruders. The barkatorium is a sun room with windows on the south, east, and west. There is a sofa under the south windows and Sam and Sarah are more than willing to share it. They prefer, however, that no one sit in the chairs near the sofa because it is harder for both of them to get into one lap. However, they are adept at making a poodle sandwich of anyone sitting on the sofa.

They greet me vocally with what strangers call a howl. I know they are talking to me, because poodles are more like people than they are like d-o-g-s. We do not say the D word in our house because it usually causes Sam and Sarah to become alert and look for the intruder. Bob Hope and his wife have five canines in their family. A reporter asked him, "I understand you have five dogs?" Bob Hope replied, "No, two dogs and three poodles."

Sam and Sarah sit on either side of me on the sofa in the evening and we visit. It is a pleasure I look forward to every day. I scratch their necks and they look at me with the kind of adoration a person gets only from a poodle. At work when asked by friends what I intend to do for fun that evening, the answer is usually, "Hug my poodles."

At the beginning and end of formal meditation repeat this exercise over several breath cycles: *Healing is taking pleasure in ordinary activities.*

Now, when you are ready, begin formal meditation.

Sit comfortably erect in your straight back chair with both feet planted on the floor. Put your hands on your legs or fold them in your lap. Breathe through your nose when you can. Close your eyes and notice your abdomen expand as you say "in" to yourself. Notice your abdomen contract as you say "out." Feel at peace as you follow your breath.

1. After meditation write this exercise on a card or piece of paper that you will look at several times today: *Healing is taking pleasure in ordinary activities.* Look at the exercise during the day and be still for a moment each time you do. Turn your attention to whatever you're doing and focus on it. Make it a ceremony.

At the end of the day write in your journal one example of using this or any exercise to achieve a shift in perception that brought with it peace of mind. Remember your Disruptions Notebook.

2. In the last few minutes of formal meditation think of something you may encounter today that is likely to evoke tension in you. Imagine that occurrence and imagine feeling tense. Imagine recognizing this tension as fear. Imagine calming yourself, turning to whatever you are doing at the time with reverence and ceremony. Feel peace.

At the very end of the meditation see clearly in your mind the picture of your goal, in addition to peace of mind,

for these eight weeks. Hold that picture. Notice the details. Feel at peace with that picture.

After meditation write this exercise on a card or piece of paper that you will look at several times today: *Healing is taking pleasure in ordinary activities*. Look at the exercise during the day and be still for a moment each time you do. When you are still, follow your breath, "in" and "out" as your abdomen rises and falls with your breath. Follow your breath through several cycles. Be at peace.

At the end of the day write in your journal one example of using this or any exercise to achieve a shift in perception that brought with it peace of mind. Remember your Disruptions Notebook.

3. In the last few minutes of formal meditation think back to a time in your past when you were very tense. Feel the full force of your tension. When your feelings are quiet remind yourself that you did not know of the option of turning to your activity of the moment as a ceremony. Imagine doing that and feeling peace.

When you are ready, let the white light build within your heart. Let it fill you and warm you. Let yourself be warmed by your bright light of forgiveness, kindness, and compassion. When you are ready let the warm, bright light spill over to another who will be healed with you.

At the very end of the meditation see clearly in your mind the picture of your goal, in addition to peace of mind, for these eight weeks. Hold that picture. Notice the details. Feel at peace with that picture.

After meditation write this exercise on a card or piece of paper that you will look at several times today: *Healing is taking pleasure in ordinary activities*. Look at the exercise during the day and be still for a moment each time you do. When you are still, follow your breath, "in" and "out" as your abdomen rises and falls with your breath. Follow your breath through several cycles. Be at peace.

At the end of the day write in your journal one example of using this or any exercise to achieve a shift in perception that brought with it peace of mind. Remember your Disruptions Notebook.

EXERCISE 6

HEALING IS STEPPING BACK AND ASKING FOR GUIDANCE.[54]

When I was in the U.S. Navy, our Chief of the Officers and Dependents Service, Rolf Steyn, was chosen to be Chief of Psychiatry at a bigger facility. Rarely had I worked with someone I admired more than Rolf Steyn. He was like a father to me, and I was distraught that he was leaving for he had taught me more about general psychiatry in one year than anyone had in my residency. When he left, I was made Acting Chief of the Officers and Dependents Service, prematurely in my estimation. However, I was put in charge of the psychiatric residents on our service, one of whom had been repeatedly criticized by the emergency room staff. They said he was rude and hostile to the patients in the emergency room. Despite his being confronted with this criticism, the resident denied his behavior. My superior, the Chief of Psychiatry, saw this as my problem, and I had better solve it, but I had no clue what to do.

Looking back on it, being able to admit that I didn't know what to do was the first step to using the force. At the time I would not have known how to identify what happened next, but after admitting to myself that I had no clue, I was open to suggestions. The suggestion came from my son, Michael, that evening at dinner. Michael was trying to figure out how our VCR worked. He asked, "Dad, do you ever use video in your work?" "No, but I should," I responded.

The next day I asked the head of the emergency room if we could videotape the resident the next time he was there and it was done. On video the resident seemed perfectly appropriate, so we made another one. On the next video he was very different. Then he was dealing with someone much closer to his age and rank who had a problem with alcohol. When I showed the resident the two videos, he was surprised but not defensive. He looked into himself and acknowledged the problem. Younger officers with alcohol problems reminded him of his brother. He was angry at his younger brother for not getting his act together and controlling his alcohol use. There were no more complaints. Looking back at that time I can identify what went right. The first step was admitting I had no idea how to solve the problem. The second step was being open to all sources for inspiration. When I am open an answer always comes.

Today, I do this formally rather than hoping to stumble on the answer. I go through all three steps. I say: 1) I have no clue what to do; 2) I will not engineer an answer but let it come to me in a moment of inspiration; 3) I trust the force.

At the beginning and end of formal meditation repeat this exercise over several breath cycles: *Healing is stepping back and asking for guidance.* When you are ready, begin formal meditation.

Sit comfortably erect in your straight back chair with both feet planted on the floor. Put your hands on your legs or fold them in your lap. Breathe through your nose when you can. Close your eyes and notice your abdomen expand as you say "in" and contract as you say "out." Feel at peace as you follow your breath.

1. After meditation write this exercise on a card or piece of paper that you will look at several times today:

Healing is stepping back and asking for guidance. Look at the exercise during the day and be still for a moment each time you do. When you experience a dilemma, admit that you don't know what to do. Ask for guidance. Be open to inspiration and trust the force.

At the end of the day write in your journal one example of using this or any exercise to achieve a shift in perception that brought with it peace of mind. Remember your Disruptions Notebook.

2. In the last few minutes of formal meditation think of something you may encounter today that is likely to confound you. Imagine that occurrence. Admit to yourself that you do not know what to do. Imagine asking for guidance, being open to inspiration, and trusting the force.

At the very end of the meditation see clearly in your mind the picture of your goal, in addition to peace of mind, for these eight weeks. Hold that picture. Notice the details. Feel at peace with that picture.

After meditation write this exercise on a card or piece of paper that you will look at several times today: *Healing is stepping back and asking for guidance.* Look at the lesson during the day and be still for a moment each time you do. When you are still, follow your breath, "in" and "out" as your abdomen rises and falls with your breath. Follow your breath through several cycles. Be at peace.

At the end of the day write in your journal one example of using this or any exercise to achieve a shift in perception that brought with it peace of mind. Remember your Disruptions Notebook.

3. In the last few minutes of formal meditation think back to a time in your past when you were confused and did not know where to turn. Feel the full force of that confusion. When your feelings are quiet remind yourself that you did not know of the option of admitting you were stumped and releasing that dilemma to the force for a solution. Imagine doing that and feeling peace.

When you are ready, let the white light build within your heart. Let it fill and warm you. Let yourself be warmed by your bright light of forgiveness, kindness, and compassion. When you are ready let that warm, bright light spill over to another who will be healed with you.

At the very end of the meditation see clearly in your mind the picture of your goal, in addition to peace of mind, for these eight weeks. Hold that picture. Notice the details. Feel at peace with that picture.

After meditation write this exercise on a card or piece of paper that you will look at several times today: *Healing is stepping back and asking for guidance.* Look at the exercise during the day and be still for a moment each time you do. When you are still, follow your breath, "in" and "out" through several cycles as your abdomen rises and falls. Be at peace.

At the end of the day write in your journal one example of using this or any exercise to achieve a shift in perception that brought with it peace of mind. Remember your Disruptions Notebook.

EXERCISE 7

MY HEALING ALLOWS OTHERS TO HEAL.[55]

Psychiatrist and author Gerald Jampolsky has done a lot to promote Attitudinal Healing. He taught me something important. Jerry and Diane Cirincione gave a workshop at Columbia Hospital in Milwaukee not long ago. Jerry does not claim to be an expert on the practice of Attitudinal Healing. He claims to struggle like everyone else.

During the two days we spent together, I saw him become quiet at times during interactions with participants. I imagined that he was tempted to react, but he recognized the impulse in himself, and instead of reacting, became quiet for a moment. I noticed that I began to do the same thing. While Jerry was healing himself from reacting too quickly, I was changing. I noticed that as I learned to be still for a moment, other people around me began to seem calmer. Calmness spreads like wildfire. It is true; I am never healed alone. The feelings I put into action change my environment and the people in it.

At the beginning and end of formal meditation repeat this exercise over several breath cycles: *My healing allows others to heal*.

Now, when you are ready, begin formal meditation.

Sit comfortably erect in your straight back chair with both feet planted on the floor. Put your hands on your legs or fold them in your lap. Breathe through your nose when you can. Close your eyes and notice your abdomen expand as you say "in" and contract as you say "out." Feel at peace as you follow your breath.

1. After meditation write this exercise on a card or piece of paper that you will look at several times today:

My healing allows others to heal. Look at the lesson during the day and be still for a moment. Each time you do, imagine your calmness spreading like wildfire.

At the end of the day write in your journal one example of using this or any exercise to achieve a shift in perception that brought with it peace of mind. Remember your Disruptions Notebook.

2. In the last few minutes of formal meditation think of something you will encounter today that is likely to make you wish to react. Imagine that occurrence. Imagine turning to your breath to calm yourself and imagine your calmness spreading like wildfire.

At the very end of the meditation see clearly in your mind the picture of your goal, in addition to peace of mind, for these eight weeks. Hold that picture. Notice the details. Feel at peace with that picture.

After meditation write this exercise on a card or piece of paper that you will look at several times today: *My healing allows others to heal.*

At the end of the day write in your journal one example of using this or any exercise to achieve a shift in perception that brought with it peace of mind. Remember your Disruptions Notebook.

3. In the last few minutes of formal meditation think back to a time in your past when you reacted rather than responded. Feel the full force of your reaction. When your feelings are quiet remind yourself that you did not know of the option of turning to your breath, calming yourself, and letting that calmness spread like wildfire. Imagine doing that and feeling peace.

When you are ready, let the white light build within

your heart. Let it fill you, and warm you. Let yourself be warmed by your bright light of forgiveness, kindness, and compassion. Then let your warm, bright light spill over to another.

At the very end of the meditation see clearly in your mind the picture of your goal, in addition to peace of mind, for these eight weeks. Hold that picture. Notice the details. Feel at peace with that picture.

After meditation write this exercise on a card or piece of paper that you will look at several times today: *My healing allows others to heal*. Look at the exercise during the day and be still for a moment each time you do. When you are still, follow your breath, "in" and "out" as your abdomen rises and falls with your breath. Follow your breath through several cycles. Be at peace.

At the end of the day write in your journal one example of using this or any exercise to achieve a shift in perception that brought with it peace of mind. Remember your Disruptions Notebook.

WEEK 6

Learning Is a Key to a Better Life. Teaching Is a Good Way to Learn.[56]

Being a good student involves being a good teacher, too. We can learn from everyone in our environment. This week we will be especially attuned to our roles as student and teacher for each other.

In addition to reading the exercises, meditating, and journaling each day, remember to write in your Disruptions Notebook any major interruptions to your peace of mind. Remember to include two important categories of detailed information: describe the villains in your disruptions and your fears in as much detail as possible.

Exercise 1

I am convinced that our children are as important as teachers for us, as we are for them. When my son, Jeff, was about 8 years old he came home from a birthday party and told me, "I had a great time, Dad! I didn't even hit anybody."

I said, "Oh, that's good."

He said, "Even when Billy pushed me."

"Um hm," I said.

He said, "I wasn't sure what to do but I asked myself *what would Elvis do?*"

Then he told me about an Elvis Presley movie, *Follow That Dream,* in which Elvis avoided violence until someone actually hit him. Similarly, Billy had not actually hit him, so Jeff did not overreact by punching him.

That day I learned a lesson I will never forget: Do not discount any sources, because you can never tell where inspiration comes from. My son taught me a valuable lesson, one that I have used over the years—to teach psychiatry with movies. One of the best sources for teaching defense mechanisms is cartoons because they are full of defense mechanisms. In fact that is what makes cartoons humorous. Has anyone ever shown more denial than Wile E. Coyote in his relentless pursuit of the Road Runner? He also shows the comic point of view, that is, anything is possible if he tries hard enough. Even though he has touched the Road Runner no longer than thirty seconds in the last thirty years he keeps trying, because he knows that with a little more effort, a little better techni-

cal support from Acme Industries, success is just a moment away.

Since I began looking closely at the movies, I have
found many lessons in them. Jeffrey has been my teacher,
and I learned from him. (I think I taught him a few things,
too.)

At the beginning and end of formal meditation repeat
this exercise over several breath cycles: *We are students
and teachers for each other.*

Now, when you are ready, begin formal meditation.

Sit comfortably erect in your straight back chair with
both feet planted on the floor. Put your hands on your legs
or fold them in your lap. Breathe through your nose when
you can. Close your eyes and notice your abdomen expand
as you say "in" and contract as you say "out." Feel at peace
as you follow your breath.

1. After meditation write this exercise on a card or
piece of paper that you will look at several times today:
We are students and teachers for each other. Look at the
exercise during the day and be still for a moment. Whenever you do, imagine learning something from each person you meet.

At the end of the day write in your journal one example of using this or any exercise to achieve a shift in perception that brought with it peace of mind. Remember
your Disruptions Notebook.

2. In the last few minutes of formal meditation think
of someone you may encounter today who may give you
an opportunity to learn. Imagine the occurrence and feel
gratitude.

At the very end of the meditation see clearly in your

mind the picture of your goal, in addition to peace of mind, for these eight weeks. Hold that picture. Notice the details. Feel at peace with that picture.

After meditation write this exercise on a card or piece of paper that you will look at several times today: *We are students and teachers for each other*. When you look at the exercise be still for a moment and follow your breath, "in" and "out" as your abdomen rises and falls. Follow your breath through several cycles. Be at peace.

At the end of the day write in your journal one example of using this or any exercise to achieve a shift in perception that brought with it peace of mind. Remember your Disruptions Notebook.

3. In the last few minutes of formal meditation think back to a time in your past when you learned an important lesson from someone. Feel the full force of your gratitude toward that person.

When you are ready, let the white light build within your heart. Let it fill and warm you. When you are ready, let your teacher be warmed by your bright light of love.

At the very end of the meditation see clearly in your mind the picture of your goal, in addition to peace of mind, for these eight weeks. Hold that picture. Notice the details. Feel at peace with that picture.

After meditation write this exercise on a card or piece of paper that you will look at several times today: *We are students and teachers for each other*. Look at the exercise during the day and be still for a moment each time you do. When you are still, follow your breath, "in" and "out" as your abdomen rises and falls with your breath. Follow your breath through several cycles. Be at peace.

At the end of the day write in your journal one example of using this or any exercise to achieve a shift in perception that brought with it peace of mind. Remember your Disruptions Notebook.

EXERCISE 2

TREAT EACH PERSON AS A PROPHET.

One of the best ways to learn from others is to treat each person as a prophet who has a lesson to teach you. In order to use this exercise, you need to have a question in mind.

Not too long ago I made up my mind to learn more about how to build a healthy exercise program into my daily life. During my meditation I vowed, "Today I want to find out more about a healthy exercise program." During the day I was talking to our Chief of Staff at Columbia Hospital, Dr. Wayne Boulanger. He always looks fit, yet he enjoys good food. At the end of our conversation, Wayne turned and walked up the stairs to the fifth floor. He had just modeled an excellent lesson in building an exercise program into one's daily life. Walk up the stairs rather than take an elevator. Later that day my friend, Jack, asked me to substitute for him in a tennis game. I agreed. Then Renée called and asked me to walk home with her. By the end of the day I had had three encounters that taught me how to build a healthy exercise program into my daily schedule. Take the stairs, walk to work, and play tennis whenever you can.

At the beginning and end of formal meditation repeat this exercise over several breath cycles: *Treat each person as a prophet.*

Now, when you are ready, begin formal meditation.

Sit comfortably erect in your straight back chair with both feet planted on the floor. Put your hands on your legs or fold them in your lap. Breathe through your nose when you can. Close your eyes and notice your abdomen expand

as you say "in" and contract as you say "out." Feel at peace as you follow your breath.

1. After meditation write this exercise on a card or piece of paper that you will look at several times today: *Treat each person as a prophet.* Look at the exercise during the day and be still for a moment. Each time you do, imagine you're learning something from each person you meet.

At the end of the day write in your journal one example of using this or any exercise to achieve a shift in perception that brought with it peace of mind. Feel gratitude toward your teachers. Remember your Disruptions Notebook.

2. In the last few minutes of formal meditation think of someone you will encounter today who may give you an opportunity to learn. Imagine the occurrence and feel gratitude toward your teacher.

At the very end of the meditation see clearly in your mind the picture of your goal, in addition to peace of mind, for these eight weeks. Hold that picture. Notice the details. Feel at peace with that picture.

After meditation write this exercise on a card or piece of paper that you will look at several times today: *Treat each person as a prophet.* Be still at intervals during the day when you read this lesson. When you are still, follow your breath, "in" and "out" as your abdomen rises and falls with your breath. Follow your breath through several cycles. Be at peace.

At the end of the day write in your journal one example of using this or any exercise to achieve a shift in per-

ception that brought with it peace of mind. Remember your Disruptions Notebook.

3. In the last few minutes of formal meditation think back to a time in your past when you learned an important lesson from someone. Feel the full force of your gratitude toward that person.

When you are ready, let the white light build within your heart. Let it fill and warm you. When you are ready, let yourself and your teacher be warmed by your bright light of love.

At the very end of the meditation see clearly in your mind the picture of your goal, in addition to peace of mind, for these eight weeks. Hold that picture. Notice the details. Feel at peace with that picture.

After meditation write this exercise on a card or piece of paper that you will look at several times today: *Treat each person as a prophet*. Look at the exercise during the day and be still for a moment each time you do. When you are still, follow your breath, "in" and "out" as your abdomen rises and falls with your breath. Follow your breath through several cycles. Be at peace.

At the end of the day write in your journal one example of using this or any exercise to achieve a shift in perception that brought with it peace of mind. Remember your Disruptions Notebook.

EXERCISE 3

JUDGING DISRUPTS LEARNING AND TEACHING.

When my younger son was about 3 years old, he announced to Renée and me that he knew what people were made of. I asked, "What are people made of?"

"Hard plastic."

I was poised to embark on a detailed lecture in cellular physiology because I judged his answer as inaccurate, but Renée asked, "How did you figure that out?" My son explained that he had been observing those plastic G.I. Joe dolls closely, and after taking several apart (that explained what happened to the missing G.I. Joes) he had a better idea about what people were made of. Renée praised him on his use of the scientific method and explained that he was very close to being right. She said that there were a few more details about people that he might be interested in and that they could read a book about it that afternoon before nap time. He said, "Good," and went back to his play.

My first impulse was to judge Jeff's hypothesis on the basis of my adult knowledge rather than to admire his use of the scientific method. My way would have undermined his learning. Renée's way enhanced it.

At the beginning and end of formal meditation repeat this exercise over several breath cycles: *Judging disrupts learning and teaching.*

Now, when you are ready, begin formal meditation.

Sit comfortably erect in your straight back chair with both feet planted on the floor. Put your hands on your legs

or fold them in your lap. Breathe through your nose when
you can. Close your eyes and notice your abdomen expand
as you say "in" and contract as you say "out." Feel at peace
as you follow your breath.

1. After meditation write this exercise on a card or
piece of paper that you will look at several times today:
Judging disrupts learning and teaching. Look at the exercise during the day and be still for a moment. Each time
you do imagine you're suspending judgment with the next
person you meet.

At the end of the day write in your journal one example of using this or any exercise to achieve a shift in perception that brought with it peace of mind. Remember
your Disruptions Notebook.

2. In the last few minutes of formal meditation think
of someone you will encounter today who may give you an
opportunity to judge. Imagine the encounter and imagine
suspending judgment and learning something from that
person.

At the very end of the meditation see clearly in your
mind the picture of your goal, in addition to peace of mind,
for these eight weeks. Hold that picture. Notice the details. Feel at peace with that picture.

After meditation write this exercise on a card or piece
of paper that you will look at several times today: *Judging disrupts learning and teaching*. Be still for a moment.
When you are still, follow your breath, "in" and "out" as
your abdomen rises and falls with your breath. Follow your
breath through several cycles. Be at peace.

At the end of the day write in your journal one example of using this or any exercise to achieve a shift in per-

ception that brought with it peace of mind. Remember
your Disruptions Notebook.

3. In the last few minutes of formal meditation think
back to your past when you learned a lesson from someone after you were able to suspend judgment, or remember a person who treated you non-judgmentally and enhanced your learning opportunity.

When you are ready, let the white light build within
your heart. Let it fill you, and warm you. Then, when you
are ready, let yourself and your teacher be warmed by your
bright light of love.

At the very end of the meditation see clearly in your
mind the picture of your goal, in addition to peace of mind,
for these eight weeks. Hold that picture. Notice the details. Feel at peace with that picture.

After meditation write this exercise on a card or piece
of paper that you will look at several times today: *Judging disrupts learning and teaching*. Be still when you read
the exercise during the day. When you are still, follow your
breath, "in" and "out" as your abdomen rises and falls with
your breath. Follow your breath through several cycles.
Be at peace.

At the end of the day write in your journal one example of using this or any exercise to achieve a shift in perception that brought with it peace of mind. Remember
your Disruptions Notebook.

I WILL TEACH WHAT I WISH TO LEARN.[58]

When I was in college at Tulane University I was afraid of flying. In a plane one sweltering summer day I sat next to a white knuckler worse than I was. On takeoff from New Orleans, as we climbed over Lake Pontchartrain, the plane lurched as the landing gear retracted. I told him, "It's no problem, the pilot is retracting the landing gear." After we leveled off, we lurched again and he again looked startled. "The pilot changed the pitch of the props," I said. When we encountered turbulence over Alabama, he became frightened again, so we just talked. During our landing in Greenville, South Carolina, he sat stiffly in his seat. "This is pretty routine . . . they always land safely," I said.

I noticed that I had been completely calm during the whole flight. On other flights, however, I had been almost as tense as my seat mate. He told me that he was a ticket agent for this airline but had not taken advantage of his opportunities to fly because of his fright. He had decided to take a chance today, and felt fortunate to sit next to me. I was pleased that I had been able to help him. What I did for him was what my father had done for me when we flew together. I had every reaction I now saw in the airline employee next to me. My father, sensing my fearfulness, explained each maneuver the pilot was making. It calmed me when my father was next to me. So, even though I had the knowledge for years, I continued to be frightened, unable to use what my father taught me until I taught it to someone else.

Today, I will teach something that I wish to learn better myself.

At the beginning and end of formal meditation repeat this exercise over several breath cycles: *I will teach what I wish to learn.*

Now, when you are ready, begin formal meditation.

Sit comfortably erect in your straight back chair with both feet planted on the floor. Put your hands on your legs or fold them in your lap. Breathe through your nose when you can. Close your eyes and notice your abdomen expand as you say "in" and contract as you say "out." Feel at peace as you follow your breath.

1. After meditation write this exercise on a card or piece of paper that you will look at several times today: *I will teach what I wish to learn.* Look at the exercise during the day and be still for a moment. Each time imagine teaching, by example, kindness, patience, and the ability to express appreciation.

At the end of the day write in your journal one example of using this or any exercise to achieve a shift in perception that brought with it peace of mind. Remember your Disruptions Notebook.

2. In the last few minutes of formal meditation think of someone you will encounter today who may give you an opportunity to show understanding rather than judgment. Imagine that occurrence. Imagine suspending judgment and teaching that person something you wish to learn better.

At the very end of the meditation see clearly in your mind the picture of your goal, in addition to peace of mind, for these eight weeks. Hold that picture. Notice the details. Feel at peace with that picture.

After meditation write this exercise on a card or piece of paper that you will look at several times today: *I will teach what I wish to learn.* Be still when you read the exercise during the day. When you are still, follow your breath, "in" and "out" as your abdomen rises and falls with your breath. Follow your breath through several cycles. Be at peace.

At the end of the day write in your journal one example of using this or any exercise to achieve a shift in perception that brought with it peace of mind. Remember your Disruptions Notebook.

3. In the last few minutes of formal meditation think back to your past when you learned from watching the behavior of someone you admired. Feel gratitude for having had an opportunity to learn from that person.

When you are ready, let the white light build within your heart. Let it fill you, and warm you. When you are ready, let yourself and your teacher be warmed by your bright light of love.

At the very end of the meditation see clearly in your mind the picture of your goal, in addition to peace of mind, for these eight weeks. Hold that picture. Notice the details. Feel at peace with that picture.

After meditation write this exercise on a card or piece of paper that you will look at several times today: *I will teach what I wish to learn.* Be still when you look at the exercise during the day. When you are still, follow your breath, "in" and "out" as your abdomen rises and falls with your breath. Follow your breath through several cycles. Be at peace.

At the end of the day write in your journal one example of using this or any exercise to achieve a shift in perception that brought with it peace of mind. Remember your Disruptions Notebook.

Exercise 5

"WHEN THE STUDENT IS READY, THE TEACHER WILL APPEAR."[59]

After the winter holidays last year I wanted to lose the weight I had gained over the previous few months. I tried all the gimmicks and programs, but they did not work for long. I was waiting for some inspiration to help me find a better way. I turned on "Larry King Live" on CNN, and the guest for the evening was Oprah Winfrey. Oprah said that she would still be heavy if she did not run five miles each day. I remembered the last time I successfully lost weight and kept it off. I had NordicTracked twenty minutes a day, every day, no matter what, in addition to changing my diet. After watching that show I returned to my old exercise program. I took off the weight and kept it off with the use of my NordicTrack. When I was ready, Oprah appeared!

At the beginning and end of formal meditation repeat this lesson over several breath cycles: *When the student is ready, the teacher will appear.* Think of a question you wish answered today.

When you are ready begin formal meditation.

Sit comfortably erect in your straight back chair with both feet planted on the floor. Put your hands on your legs or fold them in your lap. Breathe through your nose when you can. Close your eyes and notice your abdomen expand as you say "in" and contract as you say "out." Feel at peace as you follow your breath.

1. After meditation write this exercise on a card or piece of paper that you will look at several times today:

When the student is ready, the teacher will appear. Look at the exercise during the day and be still for a moment. Each time you do imagine getting an answer to your question.

At the end of the day write in your journal one example of using this or any exercise to achieve a shift in perception that brought with it peace of mind. Remember your Disruptions Notebook.

2. In the last few minutes of formal meditation think of a question you wish answered. Imagine keeping an open mind and being open to surprise when you find an answer.

At the very end of the meditation see clearly in your mind the picture of your goal, in addition to peace of mind, for these eight weeks. Hold that picture. Notice the details. Feel at peace with that picture.

After meditation write this exercise on a card or piece of paper that you will look at several times today: *When the student is ready, the teacher will appear.* Be still when you read the exercise during the day. When you are still, follow your breath, "in" and "out" as your abdomen rises and falls with your breath. Follow your breath through several cycles. Be at peace.

At the end of the day write in your journal one example of using this or any exercise to achieve a shift in perception that brought with it peace of mind. Remember your Disruptions Notebook.

3. In the last few minutes of formal meditation think back to a time in your past when you learned something really important from a chance encounter. Feel gratitude for having had an opportunity to learn from that person.

When you are ready, let the white light build within your heart. Let it fill you, and warm you. When you are ready, let yourself and your teacher be warmed by your bright light of love.

At the very end of the meditation see clearly in your mind the picture of your goal, in addition to peace of mind, for these eight weeks. Hold that picture. Notice the details. Feel at peace with that picture.

After meditation write this exercise on a card or piece of paper that you will look at several times today: *When the student is ready, the teacher will appear.* Be still when you read the exercise during the day. When you are still, follow your breath, "in" and "out" as your abdomen rises and falls with your breath. Follow your breath through several cycles. Be at peace.

At the end of the day write in your journal one example of using this or any exercise to achieve a shift in perception that brought with it peace of mind. Remember your Disruptions Notebook.

EVERYTHING THAT HAPPENS HAS A
LESSON FOR ME TO LEARN.[60]

When my younger sister was born, my mother had trouble
with the delivery and was in bed recuperating for a long
time. I went to stay with my Aunt Alma and Uncle Ted in
Grayling, Michigan. It was a cold winter. There was a lot
of snow and I was stuck indoors for long periods of time.
I missed my mother. My father was on a ship in the Pacific
and I missed him. Uncle Ted worked; Aunt Alma was busy
with housework. I was alone more than I had ever been
before.

When we were really snowed in, Uncle Ted stayed
home from work and to pass the time, he and I told each
other stories. He started the story and when he stopped I
had to provide the next installment. When I ran out of
ideas, I turned the story back to him. We spent long after-
noons cooking up the next installment of Ted, Todd, and
their trusty dog, Mr. Tubbs. We told of chasing dastardly
villains across the frozen tundra, being attacked by wolves,
and fighting the elements. We took turns leaving our he-
roes in desperate straits for the other guy to come up with
a last moment escape for Ted, Todd, and their trusty dog,
Mr. Tubbs.

Looking back at my stay in Grayling, even though it
was difficult being away from my mother, I learned something that has never left me. I became convinced that stories are a wonderful way to pass time, and that I was a
pretty good storyteller. Uncle Ted never failed to praise
my story telling, "Well, you sure are a good storyteller. I
don't know how Ted, Todd, and their trusty dog, Mr. Tubbs,

will get out of this one." I wonder if I would've been able to trust my intuition half as much without the experience of telling stories with my Uncle Ted. He taught me to relax and just let the ideas come to me.

At the beginning and end of formal meditation repeat this exercise over several breath cycles: *Everything that happens has a lesson for me to learn.*

When you are ready begin formal meditation.

First find a comfortable straight back chair. Sit erect in the chair with both feet planted on the floor. Put your hands on your legs or fold them in your lap. Breathe through your nose when you can. Close your eyes and notice your abdomen expand as you say "in" and contract as you say "out." Feel at peace as you follow your breath.

1. After meditation write this exercise on a card or piece of paper that you will look at several times today: *Everything that happens has a lesson for me to learn.* Look at the exercise during the day and be still for a moment. Each time you do, reflect on what has happened during the day and see if there has been a lesson to learn.

At the end of the day write in your journal one example of using this or any exercise to achieve a shift in perception that brought with it peace of mind. Remember your Disruptions Notebook.

2. In the last few minutes of formal meditation think of this exercise: *Everything that happens has a lesson for me to learn.* Imagine keeping an open mind and being ready to experience a lesson in everything that happens today.

At the very end of the meditation see clearly in your mind the picture of your goal, in addition to peace of mind,

for these eight weeks. Hold that picture. Notice the details. Feel at peace with that picture.

After meditation write this exercise on a card or piece of paper that you will look at several times today: *Everything that happens has a lesson for me to learn*. Be still during the day when you read your exercise. When you are still, follow your breath, "in" and "out" as your abdomen rises and falls with your breath. Follow your breath through several cycles. Be at peace.

At the end of the day write in your journal one lesson learned today. Remember your Disruptions Notebook.

3. In the last few minutes of formal meditation think back to a time in your past when you learned a lesson from an experience that you did not find all that pleasant at the time. Think of the people involved in the situation from which you learned that lesson. Feel the full force of your feelings toward these people. When the feelings have passed, move on.

When you are ready, let the white light build within your heart. Let it fill you and warm you. When you are ready, let yourself and your teachers be warmed by your bright light of love.

At the very end of the meditation see clearly in your mind the picture of your goal, in addition to peace of mind, for these eight weeks. Hold that picture. Notice the details. Feel at peace with that picture.

After meditation write this exercise on a card or piece of paper that you will look at several times today: *Everything that happens has a lesson for me to learn*. Be still for a moment when you read the exercise during the day. When you are still, follow your breath, "in" and "out" as your abdomen rises and falls with your breath. Follow your breath through several cycles. Be at peace.

At the end of the day write in your journal one lesson learned today or in the past. Remember your Disruptions Notebook.

Many times we are faced with a dilemma for which we have no answer. Sometimes we are able to find an answer, but sometimes we must put the whole question on the back burner. This means letting go of the dilemma, giving up our impulses to engineer an answer, and relying on our strong expectation that an answer will present itself when the time is right.

Marlene, a friend and facilitator of this course, was washing dishes when she noticed the smell of Ivory soap made her feel sick. She wondered why the smell affected her this way. She could not figure it out so she just put it on the back burner and asked for help from the force.

During meditation she was engulfed in rage. She felt terrified at her strong feelings, but she stayed with the feelings and an image emerged: She saw a bar of Ivory soap popping out of the water. She remembered as a child the commercial on TV in which Ivory soap popped out of the water proving that it was 99 and 99/100 percent pure because it floated. She thought that her feelings of rage were not pure and then she remembered being left with a baby sitter her mother had employed on the spur of the moment who sent her to bed without her dinner for washing the sides of the bathtub with Ivory soap. An important aspect of the story was her feeling that her mother had abandoned her to this witch of a baby sitter while she took her brothers out to have fun.

Marlene wondered why she was having this memory now. It came to her that her mother-in-law was terminally ill and she was now experiencing all the anger, hurt feelings, and rage that she had experienced with this earlier incident of abandonment even though there was only an approximate fit with the illness of her mother-in-law. She saw her mother-in-law in a new light and valued her friendship even more.

The next day, when she did the dishes, the smell of Ivory soap had no effect on her.

At the beginning and end of formal meditation repeat this exercise over several breath cycles: *When in doubt, I trust the force, my inner wisdom.* If there is something you need to figure out but cannot find an answer for, put it on the back burner.

When you are ready begin formal meditation.

Sit comfortably erect in your straight back chair with both feet planted on the floor. Put your hands on your legs or fold them in your lap. Breathe through your nose when you can. Close your eyes and notice your abdomen expand as you say "in" and contract as you say "out." Feel at peace as you follow your breath.

1. After meditation write this exercise on a card or piece of paper that you will look at several times today: *When in doubt, I trust the force, my inner wisdom.* Look at the exercise during the day. Each time be still for a moment. When you are still, follow your breath, "in" and "out" as your abdomen rises and falls with your breath. Follow your breath through several cycles. Be at peace.

At the end of the day write in your journal one example of using this or any exercise to achieve a shift in perception that brought with it peace of mind. Remember your Disruptions Notebook.

2. In the first few minutes and the last few minutes of formal meditation think of this exercise: *When in doubt, I trust the force, my inner wisdom.* Imagine keeping an open mind today and being ready to find an answer to a question for which you have no answer.

At the very end of the meditation see clearly in your mind the picture of your goal, in addition to peace of mind, for these eight weeks. Hold that picture. Notice the details. Feel at peace with that picture.

After meditation write this exercise on a card or piece of paper that you will look at several times today: *When in doubt I trust the force, my inner wisdom.* When you look at the exercise during the day, be still for a moment. When you are still, follow your breath, "in" and "out" as your abdomen rises and falls with your breath. Follow your breath through several cycles. Be at peace.

At the end of the day write in your journal one example of using this or any exercise to achieve a shift in perception that brought with it peace of mind. Remember your Disruptions Notebook.

3. In the last few minutes of formal meditation think back to a time in your past when you needed an answer, but no one seemed to help. Remember a time when you trusted yourself. Remember someone who taught you to trust yourself.

When you are ready, let the white light build within your heart. Let it fill you and warm you. When you are ready, let yourself and your teacher of self-reliance be warmed by your bright light of love.

At the very end of the meditation see clearly in your mind the picture of your goal, in addition to peace of mind,

for these eight weeks. Hold that picture. Notice the details. Feel at peace with that picture.

After meditation write this exercise on a card or piece of paper that you will look at several times today: *When in doubt I trust the force, my inner wisdom.* When you read the exercise during the day be still for a moment. When you are still, follow your breath, "in" and "out" as your abdomen rises and falls with your breath. Follow your breath through several cycles. Be at peace.

At the end of the day write in your journal one example of using this or any exercise to achieve a shift in perception that brought with it peace of mind. Remember your Disruptions Notebook.

WEEK 7

I Have an Inner Guide, the Force, which I Can Access in Quiet Moments.[62]

My reasoned intuition is available to me throughout the day if I can quiet myself and listen. In the quiet I hear the force. It does not have to be quiet outside, but I am quiet on the inside.

In addition to reading the lessons, meditating and journaling each day, remember to write in your Disruptions Notebook any major interruptions to your peace of mind this week.

EXERCISE 1

IN THE QUIET I EXPERIENCE THE FORCE.[63]

During formal meditation this morning I was using this lesson but I might have been using any lesson. Here is some of the guidance I received in between bringing myself back to my breath, that is, the rise and fall of my abdomen:

1. Allow Sarah on my lap for one dog meditation.
2. Give up trying to plan the future and enjoy holding Sarah, who is completely at home in meditation.
3. Whenever I begin to luxuriate in the process of holding Sarah, a thought of the future interrupts.
4. I must be afraid of enjoying the warmth of Sarah.
5. It was the arrival of a warm little girl—the birth of my sister—that predicated my being shipped off to the cold snows of Grayling when I was a boy.
6. Relax. I am no longer a little boy. Remember, I learned a lot from Uncle Ted in Grayling.

At the beginning and end of formal meditation repeat this exercise over several breath cycles: *In the quiet I experience the force.* If there is something you need to figure out but cannot find an answer for, put it on the back burner.

Now when you are ready begin formal meditation.

Sit comfortably erect in your straight back chair with both feet planted on the floor. Put your hands on your legs or fold them in your lap. Breathe through your nose when you can. Close your eyes and notice your abdomen expand as you say "in" and contract as you say "out." Feel at peace as you follow your breath.

1. After meditation write this exercise on a card or piece of paper that you will look at several times today: *In the quiet I experience the force*. Look at the exercise during the day and be still for a moment. When you are still, follow your breath, "in" and "out" as your abdomen rises and falls with your breath. Follow your breath through several cycles. Be at peace.

At the end of the day write in your journal one example of using this or any exercise to achieve a shift in perception that brought with it peace of mind. Remember your Disruptions Notebook.

2. In the last few minutes of formal meditation think of this exercise: *In the quiet I experience the force*. Imagine keeping an open mind today and being ready find an answer to a question for which you have no answer.

At the very end of the meditation see clearly in your mind the picture of your goal, in addition to peace of mind, for these eight weeks. Hold that picture. Notice the details. Feel at peace with that picture.

After meditation write this exercise on a card or piece of paper that you will look at several times today: *In the quiet I experience the force*. Look at the exercise during the day and be still when you do. When you are still, follow your breath, "in" and "out" as your abdomen rises and falls with your breath. Follow your breath through several cycles. Be at peace.

At the end of the day write in your journal one example of using this or any exercise to achieve a shift in perception that brought with it peace of mind. Remember your Disruptions Notebook.

3. In the last few minutes of formal meditation think back to a time when you needed an answer, but no one

seemed to help. Remember a time when you trusted yourself. Remember someone who taught you to rely on your
own judgment, or to pray, or to seek inner guidance.

When you are ready, let the white light build within
your heart. Let it fill you and warm you. When you are
ready, allow yourself and your teacher of reliance on an
inner voice be warmed by your bright light of love.

At the very end of the meditation see clearly in your
mind the picture of your goal, in addition to peace of mind,
for these eight weeks. Hold that picture. Notice the details. Feel at peace with that picture.

After meditation write this exercise on a card or piece
of paper that you will look at several times today: *In the
quiet I experience the force*. During the day when you read
the exercise, be still. When you are still, follow your breath,
"in" and "out" as your abdomen rises and falls with your
breath. Follow your breath through several cycles. Be at
peace.

At the end of the day write in your journal one example of using this or any exercise to achieve a shift in perception that brought with it peace of mind. Remember
your Disruptions Notebook.

Exercise 2

**NOW—THE ONLY TIME I HAVE—
I TRUST THE FORCE.**

Here is a lesson I taught myself. First, I worry for a moment. When I worry, I am thinking about the future. Then I feel depressed for a moment. When I feel depressed, I am thinking about the past. Then I feel ashamed for a moment. When I feel ashamed, I am thinking about the past with the idea that others are looking down on me. When I worry, I am thinking about the future. When I feel depressed or ashamed, I am thinking about the past. So when I feel unhappy I am projecting myself into a time that is either not yet here or has already passed. It is being with the now that I experience the force. When I experience the force, I recognize that the past is gone and the future is not here. Now is the only time there is, and in this time I have everything that I need.

Try it for yourself. When you worry, you are thinking about the future. When you are depressed or ashamed, you are thinking about the past. Turn back to your breath. When you do, you are thinking about the present. The present is perfect.

At the beginning and end of formal meditation repeat this exercise over several breath cycles: *Now—the only time I have—I trust the force.* If there is something you need to figure out but cannot find an answer for, put it on the back burner.

Sit comfortably erect in your straight back chair with both feet planted on the floor. Put your hands on your legs or fold them in your lap. Breathe through your nose when you can. Close your eyes and notice your abdomen expand

as you say "in" and contract as you say "out." Feel at peace as you follow your breath.

1. After meditation write this exercise on a card or piece of paper that you will look at several times today: *Now—the only time I have—I trust the force*. Look at the exercise during the day and be still for a moment. Focus on the moment. Each time you do, feel peace.

At the end of the day write in your journal one example of using this lesson or any other to achieve a shift in perception that brought with it peace of mind. Remember your Disruptions Notebook.

2. In the last few minutes of formal meditation think of this exercise: *Now—the only time I have—I trust the force*. Imagine keeping an open mind today and being ready find an answer to a question for which you have no answer.

At the very end of the meditation see clearly in your mind the picture of your goal, in addition to peace of mind, for these eight weeks. Hold that picture. Notice the details. Feel at peace with that picture.

After meditation write this exercise on a card or piece of paper that you will look at several times today: *Now—the only time I have—I trust the force*. During the day when you read the exercise, be still for a moment. When you are still, follow your breath, "in" and "out" as your abdomen rises and falls with your breath. Follow your breath through several cycles. Be at peace.

At the end of the day write in your journal one example of using this or any exercise to achieve a shift in perception that brought with it peace of mind. Remember your Disruptions Notebook.

3. In the last few minutes of formal meditation think back to a time in your past when you needed an answer, but no one seemed to help. Remember a time you trusted yourself. Remember someone who taught you to trust yourself.

When you are ready, let the white light build within your heart. Let it fill you and warm you. After a few moments let you and your teacher of reliance on your inner guidance be warmed by your bright light of love.

At the very end of the meditation see clearly in your mind the picture of your goal, in addition to peace of mind, for these eight weeks. Hold that picture. Notice the details. Feel at peace with that picture.

After meditation write this exercise on a card or piece of paper that you will look at several times today: *Now— the only time I have—I trust the force.* During the day be still for a moment when you read your exercise. When you are still, follow your breath, "in" and "out" as your abdomen rises and falls with your breath. Follow your breath through several cycles. Be at peace.

At the end of the day write in your journal one example of using this or any exercise to achieve a shift in perception that brought with it peace of mind. Remember your Disruptions Notebook.

WITH THE FORCE,
FEAR IS UNNECESSARY.[64]

What is the worst thing that could happen? I could be hit by a train and die. How do I know that would be bad? I can see so little of the known matter, information, and energy around me that what I think of as death may be life, and what I think of as life may be death, by comparison. I do not know; I cannot know.

My friend, Sandy Abend, told me this joke. Fred and Sophie, a couple in their eighties, were killed in a car accident. At the pearly gates they were met by the gatekeeper who told them the following: "Well, Fred, welcome to heaven. I see from your records that while on earth you enjoyed playing golf. It usually takes a while to process your papers before I can show you to your accommodations, so maybe you would like to play a round of golf. May I recommend the Angel Gate course. It is a par 72 with a slope rating of 131. You might enjoy playing it from the white tees."

Then turning to Sophie, the gatekeeper said, "Sophie, I see from your records that you kept the family afloat financially by your astute commodity trading. May I recommend the Blue Sky Commodity Exchange? There is a monorail that will take you directly there."

Sophie left for the Exchange and Fred proceeded to the Angel Gate course, where the starter matched him with three players of equal talent. Fred had his best round in years. He shot a 76. He went back to the pearly gates. Sophie was still at the Exchange. The gatekeeper told him that it would be a little while longer and he might want to try the Lucifer's Languish course, a Pete Dye track with a par of 74 and a slope rating of 192. Fred left, played the most difficult golf course in the time-space continuum, and scored a 72. He went back to the pearly gates elated. There was Sophie clutching her profits from trading winter wheat, ecstatic that she had doubled her money in one afternoon. She asked Fred how he had enjoyed his golf and he said: "The golf was wonderful! I only have one complaint, Sophie. Do you remember how you talked me into eating a low cholesterol diet for the last forty years so we would live longer?"

At the beginning and end of formal meditation repeat this exercise over several breath cycles: *With the force, fear is unnecessary.* If there is something you need to figure out but cannot find an answer for, put it on the back burner where the force works on things.

Sit comfortably erect in your straight back chair with both feet planted on the floor. Put your hands on your legs or fold them in your lap. Close your eyes and notice your abdomen expand as you say "in" and contract as you say "out." Feel at peace as you follow your breath.

1. After meditation write this exercise on a card or piece of paper that you will look at several times today: *With the force, fear is unnecessary.* Look at the exercise during the day and be still for a moment. Focus on the moment. Each time you do, feel peace.

At the end of the day write in your journal one example of using this or any exercise to achieve a shift in perception that brought with it peace of mind. Remember your Disruptions Notebook.

2. In the last few minutes of formal meditation imagine something that you may encounter in your life today that stimulates fear in you. Think of the exercise: *With the force, fear is unnecessary.*

At the very end of the meditation see clearly in your mind the picture of your goal, in addition to peace of mind, for these eight weeks. Hold that picture. Notice the details. Feel at peace with that picture.

After meditation write this exercise on a card or piece of paper that you will look at several times today: *With the force, fear is unnecessary.* Be still when you think of the exercise during the day. When you are still, follow your breath, "in" and "out" as your abdomen rises and falls with your breath. Follow your breath through several cycles. Be at peace.

At the end of the day write in your journal one moment that you dealt with fear effectively by using this or any exercise. Remember your Disruptions Notebook.

3. In the last few minutes of formal meditation think back to a time in your past when you were frightened. Remember how the fear worked out. If there was someone who helped you overcome your fear, remember that person with gratitude.

When you are ready, let the white light build within your heart. Let it fill you and warm you. When you feel ready, let you and the other person be warmed by your bright light of love.

At the very end of the meditation see clearly in your mind the picture of your goal, in addition to peace of mind, for these eight weeks. Hold that picture. Notice the details. Feel at peace with that picture.

After meditation write this exercise on a card or piece of paper that you will look at several times today: *With the force, fear is unnecessary.* Be still when you think of your exercise during the day. When you are still, follow your breath, "in" and "out" as your abdomen rises and falls with your breath. Follow your breath through several cycles. Be at peace.

At the end of the day write in your journal one moment that you dealt with fear effectively by using this or any exercise. Remember your Disruptions Notebook.

EXERCISE 4

THE FORCE LOOKS THROUGH ME.[65]

One of my functions is to be an emissary of the force, to be a love finder rather than a fault finder, to bring peace, joy, love, and forgiveness to those around me. With the force as my guide there is no human action that cannot be done mindfully, with reverence.

When my children were young, I promised that we would do something special on an upcoming Saturday morning. When the day arrived, I had no real plan, so I relied on my inner guide. I gathered them around and told them that today we were going to clean the spots off the living room rug. They thought that would be exciting when they saw that each had his very own plastic spray bottle of cleaner and a small bucket of water with a brush.

Together we went after the spots on the living room rug. We were having such a great time working together that Renée joined in. Together as a family we sprayed, scrubbed, rubbed and patted the spots on the living room rug. My son, Michael, was an especially adept spot remover. We had a great time and it was not too long before many of the spots were gone.

A few weeks later, when I was at work, Renée asked the kids what they wanted to do for fun. They had been giving this some thought and had talked it over among themselves. Michael said, "Let's remove the spots from the dining room rug."

Looking back I remember that as one of the best times we had as a family. We worked together. I can see remnants of that joy when I watch my wife and children today working at projects they like to do. The force looks through me today by finding ways to bring people together in every-day activities.

When you are ready begin formal meditation. In the first and last few breath cycles say to yourself: *The force looks through me.*

Sit comfortably erect in your straight back chair with both feet planted on the floor. Put your hands on your legs or fold them in your lap. Breathe through your nose when you can. Close your eyes and notice your abdomen expand as you say "in" and contract as you say "out." Feel at peace as you follow your breath.

1. After meditation write this exercise on a card or piece of paper that you will look at several times today: *The force looks through me.* If you should lose your feelings of confidence, pleasure, respect, and reverence at any time today, be still for a moment and look at the lesson. Focus on the moment. Each time you do, feel peace return.

At the end of the day write in your journal one example of using this or any exercise to achieve a shift in perception that brought with it peace of mind. Remember your Disruptions Notebook.

2. In the last few minutes of formal meditation imagine something that you may encounter in your life today that stimulates fear in you. Think of the exercise today: *The force looks through me.* Imagine calming yourself, remembering that you are an emissary of the force. Feel confidence, pleasure, respect, and reverence return.

At the very end of the meditation see clearly in your mind the picture of your goal, in addition to peace of mind, for these eight weeks. Hold that picture. Notice the details. Feel at peace with that picture.

After meditation write this exercise on a card or piece of paper that you will look at several times today: *The force looks through me*. During the day when you read your exercise, be still for a moment. When you are still, follow your breath, "in" and "out" as your abdomen rises and falls with your breath. Follow your breath through several cycles. Be at peace.

At the end of the day write in your journal one example of using this or any exercise to achieve a shift in perception that brought with it peace of mind. Remember your Disruptions Notebook.

3. In the last few minutes of formal meditation think back to a time in your past when you enjoyed a simple activity like sitting on the beach, fishing, washing the dishes, scrubbing the floor. Remember the feelings of oneness, confidence, pleasure, and respect that accompany such an activity. If there was someone who helped you achieve this pleasure, remember that person with gratitude.

When you are ready, let the white light build within your heart. Let it fill you and warm you. When you feel ready, let yourself and the other person be warmed by your bright light of love.

At the very end of the meditation see clearly in your mind the picture of your goal, in addition to peace of mind, for these eight weeks. Hold that picture. Notice the details. Feel at peace with that picture.

After meditation write this exercise on a card or piece of paper that you will look at several times today: *The force looks through me*. During the day when you read the exercise, be still for a moment. When you are still, follow your breath, "in" and "out" as your abdomen rises and falls with your breath. Follow your breath through several cycles. Be at peace.

At the end of the day write in your journal one example of using this or any exercise to achieve a shift in perception that brought with it peace of mind. Remember your Disruptions Notebook.

Exercise 5

WHEN I AM STILL,
I HEAR THE QUIET VOICE.[66]

One of the real confidence builders in life is knowing that any time I can be still for a moment, I can get in touch with my inner wisdom. My inner wisdom is a quiet voice that needs stillness to get through to me. It does not have to be still outside, only inside me. If I wish, I could live the whole day in touch with my inner guide. This is excellent practice and increases my confidence that I can access the force at will. Such a day is a day of mindfulness. Mindfulness is living in the present with planned grace and a sense of ceremony that celebrates the only time we have: now.

When I awoke, I meditated for twenty minutes. At the end of that time I thought of this lesson and decided that every step I'd take that day would be with awareness and ceremony. In my stillness I could experience the force. I showered slowly, then dressed with a sense of ceremony. I walked to Columbia Hospital slowly, seeing the path, the snow, the footsteps that I was walking in. I counted my out-breaths. I walked through the University of Wisconsin campus and I observed the quadrangle and the Golda Meir Library. I noticed the people and smiled at each one as I passed them and said "good morning."

In the hospital I noticed the shining, polished floors, the warm walls, and the framed prints on them. I walked up the stairs to my office on the eighth floor and picked up the mail. Then, mindfully, I retraced my steps. At home I built a fire in the fireplace, talked to Renée, hugged Sam and Sarah, and read the paper, being aware of my breath and staying calm and centered. At lunchtime I prepared sandwiches and tea. I made a special effort to be with Renée, attentive and aware as we talked.

In the afternoon I did some reading, then cleaned my closet, not with the focus on finishing but on enjoying the process. Each hour, on the hour, I looked at the exercise for the day: *When I am still, I hear the quiet voice.* I was still for a minute, followed my breath, and listened for inspiration. All my inner guidance pointed toward continuing what I was doing. I followed this process through dinner. After dinner I washed the dishes slowly with no thought of finishing. At the end of the day I recorded in my journal a moment during the day that I turned away from frustration and found peace.

The moment I recorded came during the time I was reading a novel on our bed. Sam joined me and lay on my left side. Sarah climbed up on my right side. Sarah objected to my paying more attention to my book than to her by putting her head on my chest between my face and the book. I felt annoyed for a moment, then I remembered that peace was a choice I had made and I put down the book and captured this special moment by giving my dogs a big hug. We meditated together for a moment. When I was ready, I turned back to my book. Neither dog objected. They lay beside me as I read.

At the beginning and end of formal meditation repeat this exercise over several breath cycles: *When I am still, I hear the quiet voice.* Make sure that you bring pleasure, confidence, respect, and reverence with you wherever you go today.

When you are ready begin formal meditation.

Sit comfortably erect in your straight back chair with both feet planted on the floor. Put your hands on your legs

or fold them in your lap. Breathe through your nose when you can. Close your eyes and notice your abdomen expand as you say "in" and contract as you say "out." Feel at peace as you follow your breath.

1. After meditation write this exercise on a card or piece of paper that you will look at several times today: *When I am still, I hear the quiet voice.* If you should lose your feelings of confidence, pleasure, respect and reverence at any time today, be still for a moment, look at the exercise. Focus on the moment. Each time you do, feel peace return.

At the end of the day write in your journal one example of using this or any exercise to achieve a shift in perception that brought with it peace of mind. Remember your Disruptions Notebook.

2. In the last few minutes of formal meditation imagine something that you may encounter in your life today that might stimulate annoyance in you. Think of the exercise today: *When I am still, I hear the quiet voice.* Imagine calming yourself, remembering that you can access the force at any moment you decide to be still. Feel confidence, pleasure, respect, and reverence return.

At the very end of the meditation see clearly in your mind the picture of your goal, in addition to peace of mind, for these eight weeks. Hold that picture. Notice the details. Feel at peace with that picture.

After meditation write this exercise on a card or piece of paper that you will look at several times today: *When I am still, I hear the quiet voice.* During the day be still for a moment when you read your exercise. When you are still, follow your breath, "in" and "out" as your abdomen rises and falls with your breath. Follow your breath through several cycles. Be at peace.

At the end of the day write in your journal one instance when you dealt with annoyance effectively by using this or any exercise. Remember your Disruptions Notebook.

3. In the last few minutes of formal meditation think back to a time in your past when you enjoyed a simple activity like sitting on the beach, fishing, washing the dishes, scrubbing the floor. Remember the feelings of oneness, confidence, pleasure, and respect that accompanied such a moment. If there was someone who helped you achieve this pleasure, remember that person with gratitude.

When you are ready, let the white light build within your heart. Let it fill you and warm you. When you feel ready, let yourself and the other person be warmed by your bright light of love.

At the very end of the meditation see clearly in your mind the picture of your goal, in addition to peace of mind, for these eight weeks. Hold that picture. Notice the details. Feel at peace with that picture.

After meditation write this exercise on a card or piece of paper that you will look at several times today: *When I am still, I hear the quiet voice.* During the day when you read your exercise, be still for a moment. When you are still, follow your breath "in" and "out" as your abdomen rises and falls with your breath. Follow your breath through several cycles. Be at peace.

At the end of the day write in your journal one instance when you applied this exercise. Remember your Disruptions Notebook.

AS FOR THE FUTURE,
I TRUST THE FORCE.[67]

An old saying goes, "Man plans and the gods laugh." We are not very good at planning the future. We can choose a general direction but the details may be left to the force.

During the times I planned fishing trips with my grandfather I asked him a lot of questions about his life. I knew that he had been a star athlete in high school and I wondered how that influenced his life. He said that it had led to his first career. He had not planned it but because he was pretty well known in the small town where he grew up, he was asked to play in the band that went into saloons to play religious music and turn the saloon goers away from the demon rum. That led him to become an orchestra leader, an occupation that never went over well with his family. I asked him how it had felt to be an orchestra leader. He said that he was frightened at first because he had no formal musical training, but he just had a feeling for it. He managed to teach himself to play every instrument in the orchestra. Then, he said, he became a car dealer. I asked him if he knew anything about cars. He said no, but he had a feeling for it. Without a plan my grandfather became a very accomplished person. He just followed what he had a feeling for. I think that is what we might call trusting the force.

At the beginning and end of formal meditation repeat this exercise over several breath cycles: *As for the future, I trust the force.* Make sure that you bring pleasure, confidence, respect and reverence with you wherever you go today. Do not worry about results. Put results in the hands of the force.

When you are ready begin formal meditation.

Sit comfortably erect in your straight back chair with both feet planted on the floor. Put your hands on your legs or fold them in your lap. Breathe through your nose when you can. Close your eyes and notice your abdomen expand as you say "in" and contract as you say "out." Feel at peace as you follow your breath.

1. After meditation write this exercise on a card or piece of paper that you will look at several times today: *As for the future, I trust the force.* If you should lose your feelings of confidence, pleasure, respect, and reverence at any time today, be still for a moment, and look at the lesson. Focus on the moment. Each time you do, feel peace return.

At the end of the day write in your journal one example of using this or any exercise to achieve a shift in perception that brought with it peace of mind. Remember your Disruptions Notebook.

2. In the last few minutes of formal meditation imagine something that you may encounter in your life today that might stimulate annoyance. Think of the exercise today: *As for the future, I trust the force.* Imagine calming yourself, remembering that you can access the force at any moment you decide to be still. Feel confidence and put the results in the hands of the force.

At the very end of the meditation see clearly in your mind the picture of your goal, in addition to peace of mind, for these eight weeks. Hold that picture. Notice the details. Feel at peace with that picture.

After meditation write this exercise on a card or piece of paper that you will look at several times today: *As for the future, I trust the force.* When you read your exercise during the day, be still for a moment. When you are still, follow your breath, "in" and "out" as your abdomen rises and falls with your breath. Follow your breath through several cycles. Be at peace.

At the end of the day write in your journal one example of using this or any exercise to achieve a shift in perception that brought with it peace of mind. Remember your Disruptions Notebook.

3. In the last few minutes of formal meditation think back to a time in your past when you did not worry so much about the outcome of an activity but just trusted yourself. If there was someone who helped you achieve this sense of confidence remember that person with gratitude.

When you are ready, let the white light build within your heart. Let it fill you and warm you. When you feel ready, let yourself and the other person be warmed by your bright light of love.

At the very end of the meditation see clearly in your mind the picture of your goal, in addition to peace of mind, for these eight weeks. Hold that picture. Notice the details. Feel at peace with that picture.

After meditation write this exercise on a card or piece of paper that you will look at several times today: *As for the future, I trust the force.* Be still for a moment during the day when you read your exercise. When you are still, follow your breath, "in" and "out" as your abdomen rises and falls with your breath. Follow your breath through several cycles. Be at peace.

At the end of the day write in your journal one example of using this or any exercise to achieve a shift in perception that brought with it peace of mind. Remember your Disruptions Notebook.

IF I SURRENDER CONTROL,
THE FORCE WILL LEAD THE WAY. [68]

If there is one exercise that encompasses everything in Attitudinal Healing it is this one. At every step during the day, at every crossroads, at every decision point, I can step back and let the force lead the way.

Three years ago we were planning a Behavioral Medicine Service at Columbia Hospital. Behavioral Medicine provides mental health services adjunctive to surgery, medicine, family practice, obstetrics, and gynecology. These services provide stress management strategies for psychiatric consultation and treatment. It means helping people frightened by illness or even by the thought of illness. I knew that we needed an approach that would allow the principles of mental health to be applied in bite-sized portions to any and all health care problems, but I had no clue how to develop such an approach. Jann McClintock, a clinical nurse-specialist in psychiatry, was working with me. We were stumped, but were determined to find a way.

During that week I stumbled across a big, thick blue book in Jann's office, *A Course in Miracles*. Using this book we formed a study group for anyone who wanted to study with us. We used the guidelines provided by the Foundation for Inner Peace, the book's publisher. After a year there were thirty people from the hospital and surrounding neighborhood studying with us. I was amazed at what good sense the *Course* made psychologically. However, the Christian language in the book put off a few people despite the fact that all the terms may be seen as metaphors. Luckily, we found *Love is the Answer* by Gerald Jampolsky, M.D. and Diane Cirincione that provided the necessary non-denominational introduction. It was sensational!

Last year Columbia Hospital invited Jerry and Diane to give our annual Psychiatry Conference and it was the best attended conference in our history. We are a very traditional hospital, with a Department of Psychiatry that is also quite conservative. So it was no mean feat to introduce Attitudinal Healing. But we knew the time had come for a cost-conscious adjunct to individual psychotherapy. What makes it such a bargain is that the patients who choose to attend our Attitudinal Healing groups pay only a small fee for the Introductory Course. The groups are free.

Jerry and Diane have helped guide us through implementing Attitudinal Healing in our hospital. They even sent us a helper, Marilyn Robinson, to teach our group facilitators and have stayed in touch and provided inspiration and guidance to us. We are eternally grateful for their kindness. Today, Attitudinal Healing is the core to all our Behavioral Medicine programs. It came about by stepping back and letting the force lead the way.

At the beginning and end of formal meditation repeat this exercise over several breath cycles: *If I surrender control, the force will lead the way.* Make sure that you bring pleasure, confidence, respect, and reverence with you wherever you go today. Do not worry about direction. Put direction in the hands of the force.

When you are ready begin formal meditation.

Sit comfortably erect in your straight back chair with both feet planted on the floor. Put your hands on your legs or fold them in your lap. Breathe through your nose when you can. Close your eyes and notice your abdomen expand as you say "in" and contract as you say "out." Feel at peace as you follow your breath.

1. After meditation write this exercise on a card or piece of paper that you will look at several times today: *If I surrender control, the force will lead the way*. If you should lose your sense of direction today, be still for a moment and look at the exercise. Focus on the moment. Each time you do, feel peace return.

At the end of the day write in your journal one example of using this or any exercise to achieve a shift in perception that brought with it peace of mind. Remember your Disruptions Notebook.

2. In the last few minutes of formal meditation imagine something that you may encounter in your life today that might confound you. Think of the exercise today: *If I surrender control, the force will lead the way*. Imagine calming yourself, remembering that you can access the force at any moment you decide to be still. Feel confidence and put direction in the hands of the force.

At the very end of the meditation see clearly in your mind the picture of your goal, in addition to peace of mind, for these eight weeks. Hold that picture. Notice the details. Feel at peace with that picture.

After meditation write this exercise on a card or piece of paper that you will look at several times today: *If I surrender control, the force will lead the way*. When you read your exercise during the day, be still for a moment. When you are still, follow your breath, "in" and "out" as your abdomen rises and falls with your breath. Follow your breath through several cycles. Be at peace.

At the end of the day write in your journal one example of using this or any exercise to achieve a shift in perception that brought with it peace of mind. Remember your Disruptions Notebook.

3. In the last few minutes of formal meditation think back to a time in your past when you did not worry so much about direction, but just trusted yourself. If there was someone who helped you achieve this sense of confidence remember that person with gratitude.

When you are ready, let the white light build within your heart. Let it fill you and warm you. When you feel ready, let yourself and the other person be warmed by your bright light of love.

At the very end of the meditation see clearly in your mind the picture of your goal, in addition to peace of mind, for these eight weeks. Hold that picture. Notice the details. Feel at peace with that picture.

After meditation write this exercise on a card or piece of paper that you will look at several times today: *If I surrender control, the force will lead the way*. During the day when you read your exercise, be still for a moment. When you are still, follow your breath, "in" and "out" as your abdomen rises and falls with your breath. Follow your breath through several cycles. Be at peace.

At the end of the day write in your journal one example of using this or any exercise to achieve a shift in perception that brought with it peace of mind. Remember your Disruptions Notebook.

WEEK 8

There Is a Better Way to See the World.[69]

This week all the exercises are the headlines from previous weeks. These are seven elements of Attitudinal Healing. The first one is the foundation and all the rest build on it. In addition to reading the exercises, meditating, and journaling each day, remember to write in your Disruptions Notebook any major interruptions to your peace of mind this week.

Exercise 1

THINGS ARE NOT AS I SEE THEM NOW, LEAST OF ALL WHAT IS BEST FOR ME.[70]

When I was in the Navy, I became impressed by what little I see and how little of my own interest I apprehend. Of the invisible forces that influenced my life and others, totally out of sight was the power of the secret.

One of the challenges of being at Bethesda Naval Hospital was that we were helping people with secrets. I never understood how devastating to a family and a marriage a secret can be until I practiced there. Often, almost by accident I learned that someone had a secret. Often it was not a secret lover or liaison but a secret in his work. Frequently we were able to trace the beginning of a personal conflict to a time when a conflict at work set up a quandary in one marriage partner.

As one person said in private, "How do I tell my wife that I think my commanding officer is one brick short in the way he is handling our early warning radar when I am not even supposed to mention that I work in radar or that I have anything to do with the early warning system?" From not being able to talk with his wife about this worry, he found other related areas hard to talk about and soon was not talking about work at all. Now, a major area of his life was off limits. He began hanging around after work with the guys who could talk about their work, and a rift developed in the marriage. He and his wife argued more and more and he began drinking more. He saw trouble and came for help.

In my work I do not talk about patients at home. Early in our marriage Renée asked me, "What did you do today?" "Worked," I responded. End of conversation.

Later I learned that the most secret work can be discussed by analogy. For example my radar officer learned to tell his wife, "I am having a hard time at work because our group is not pulling in the same direction. It's like this: suppose we were a baseball team and the catcher insisted on setting up with his back to the pitcher. The rest of the team might be playing very well, but each ball the hitter misses thumps the catcher in the back. Even though this is happening, the catcher insists that this is the proper position and since he is the captain of the team, no one can overrule him." His wife could then respond, "No wonder you feel grumpy. I would feel that way, too." She could understand his feelings.

I could say to Renée, "I worked on this interesting baseball problem. There was this dispute in management about how the catcher should line up and everyone thought it had to go unspoken. The secret feelings were wrecking the third baseman's marriage. Once he could talk about the feelings, it began to heal, even though the dispute in management is yet unresolved."

Unspoken secrets wreck relationships. They are not something we see. Nor do we see the havoc they wreak. Secrets cause problems within ourselves when we have memories or feelings we cannot face.

At the beginning and end of formal meditation repeat this exercise over several breath cycles: *Things are not as I see them now, least of all what is best for me.* Make sure that you find a way to talk to yourself and loved ones today openly, without secrets.

When you are ready, begin formal meditation.

Sit comfortably erect in your straight back chair with both feet planted on the floor. Put your hands on your legs or fold them in your lap. Breathe through your nose when you can. Close your eyes and notice your abdomen expand

as you say "in" and contract as you say "out." Feel at peace as you follow your breath.

1. After meditation write this exercise on a card or piece of paper that you will look at several times today: *Things are not as I see them now, least of all what is best for me.* If you should lose your feelings of confidence, pleasure, respect, and reverence at any time today, be still for a moment, look at the exercise. Focus on the moment. Each time you do, feel peace return.

At the end of the day write in your journal one example of using this or any exercise to achieve a shift in perception that brought with it peace of mind. Remember your Disruptions Notebook.

2. In the last few minutes of formal meditation imagine something that you may encounter in your life today that might stimulate a need for secrecy. Think of the exercise today: *Things are not as I see them now, least of all what is best for me.* Open yourself and remember you can access the force at any moment you decide to be still. Feel confidence, pleasure, respect, and reverence return.

At the very end of the meditation see clearly in your mind the picture of your goal, in addition to peace of mind, for these eight weeks. Hold that picture. Notice the details. Feel at peace with that picture.

After meditation write this exercise on a card or piece of paper that you will look at several times today: *Things are not as I see them now, least of all what is best for me.* Be still during the day when you read your exercise. When you are still, follow your breath, "in" and "out" as your abdomen rises and falls with your breath. Follow your breath through several cycles. Be at peace.

At the end of the day write in your journal one example of using this or any exercise to achieve a shift in perception that brought with it peace of mind. Remember your Disruptions Notebook.

3. In the last few minutes of formal meditation think back to a time in your past when you enjoyed a moment of openness with someone who accepted you for just who you are. Remember the feelings of oneness, confidence, pleasure, and respect that accompany such a moment. Remember with gratitude the person who helped you achieve this pleasure.

When you are ready, let the white light build within your heart. Let it fill you and warm you. When you are thoroughly warmed by the light, let yourself and the other person be warmed by your bright light of love.

At the very end of the meditation see clearly in your mind the picture of your goal, in addition to peace of mind, for these eight weeks. Hold that picture. Notice the details. Feel at peace with that picture.

After meditation write this exercise on a card or piece of paper that you will look at several times today: *Things are not as I see them now, least of all what is best for me.* Be still for a moment during the day when you read your exercise. When you are still, follow your breath, "in" and "out" as your abdomen rises and falls with your breath. Follow your breath through several cycles. Be at peace.

At the end of the day write in your journal one example of using this or any exercise to achieve a shift in perception that brought with it peace of mind. Remember your Disruptions Notebook.

ALL EMOTIONS MAY BE VIEWED AS EITHER LOVE OR FEAR.[71]

The first principle of Attitudinal Healing is that the essence of my being is love. Whenever I am not feeling loving kindness, I am afraid. Fear takes many forms. When I am afraid, I compensate by becoming very certain. When I am afraid, I feel stressed. When I am afraid, I find fault. When I am afraid, I feel angry. When I am afraid, I feel guilty and ashamed. When I am afraid, I see myself as separate from others. When I am afraid, I feel meaninglessness. When I am afraid, I feel attached to outcomes, things, being right, being great, being loved, and being rich. When I am afraid to feel angry at someone, I feel hurt.

I can overcome all this fear by stepping back and listening to myself and others with loving kindness rather than judgment. I can do this if I keep my eye on my primary goal:

Peace of Mind

When I first started trying to apply Attitudinal Healing principles, I found that I was doing fine, but others were not practicing the principles with the same fervor as I was. I felt sure that when I was the less guilty one in a misunderstanding, that the more guilty person would have to change in order for me to have peace of mind. Not only was I certain about that, but if I were to interview 100 people on the street, I was certain that the majority of them would agree with me.

One Monday morning Renée left the house before I

did. She took my keys, which meant that I could not drive my car to a meeting across town. Clearly this irresponsible behavior would have to be reversed and paid for if I were going to have peace of mind. The subject of which one was more guilty need not even be raised. The prosecution rests; no jury could disagree with me.

It did not occur to me to look at this as a message from providence that maybe my attention might have been better applied elsewhere that morning. I did not recognize my certainty as fearfulness. I did not realize that part of my story was to show how this inferior female person (my younger sister who was kept close to my mother when I was sent to Grayling in an incalculable miscarriage of justice?) was never going to be my equal in responsibility. I did not see myself as contemptuously superior— merely superior. Then I read that Anwar Sadat considered the people who imprisoned him as his greatest teachers because they gave him the greatest opportunities to forgive. Maybe I was missing a thing or two.

Slowly I began to get it. My frightened-self emerged during those times when I saw myself as the less guilty one in a misunderstanding. I did not have to prove myself the superior one. All I had to do was feel anger and then when those feelings passed, let go of them. Letting go of blame is forgiveness. Then my loving self could re-emerge. A shorthand question I can ask myself is, "Do I want to be right or do I want peace of mind?"

At the beginning and end of formal meditation repeat this exercise over several breath cycles: *All emotions may be viewed as either love or fear.*

When you are ready, begin formal meditation.

Sit comfortably erect in your straight back chair with both feet planted on the floor. Put your hands on your legs

or fold them in your lap. Breathe through your nose when you can. Close your eyes and notice your abdomen expand as you say "in" and contract as you say "out." Feel at peace as you follow your breath.

1. After meditation write this exercise on a card or piece of paper that you will look at several times today: *All emotions may be viewed as either love or fear*. If you should lose your feelings of confidence, pleasure, respect and reverence at any time today, be still for a moment, look at the exercise. Focus on the moment. Each time you do, feel peace return.

At the end of the day write in your journal one example of using this or any exercise to achieve a shift in perception that brought with it peace of mind. Remember your Disruptions Notebook.

2. In the last few minutes of formal meditation imagine something that you may encounter in your life today that might stimulate fear in you. Think of today's exercise: *All emotions may be viewed as either love or fear*. Open yourself, remembering that you can access the force at any moment you decide to be still. Feel confidence, pleasure, respect, and reverence return.

At the very end of the meditation see clearly in your mind the picture of your goal, in addition to peace of mind, for these eight weeks. Hold that picture. Notice the details. Feel at peace with that picture.

After meditation write this exercise on a card or piece of paper that you will look at several times today: *All emotions may be viewed as either love or fear*. Be still during the day when you read your exercise. When you are still, follow your breath, "in" and "out" as your abdomen rises and falls with your breath. Follow your breath through several cycles. Be at peace.

At the end of the day write one moment that you dealt with annoyance effectively by using this or any exercise. Remember your Disruptions Notebook.

3. In the last few minutes of formal meditation think back to a time in your past when you enjoyed a moment of openness with someone when you accepted her for being just who she was. Remember the feelings of oneness, confidence, pleasure, and respect that accompanied such a moment. Remember with gratitude the person who gave you the opportunity to share this moment.

When you are ready, let the white light build within your heart. Let it fill you and warm you. When you feel ready, let yourself and the other person be warmed by your bright light of love.

At the very end of the meditation see clearly in your mind the picture of your goal, in addition to peace of mind, for these eight weeks. Hold that picture. Notice the details. Feel at peace with that picture.

After meditation write this exercise on a card or piece of paper that you will look at several times today: *All emotions may be viewed as either love or fear*. Each time you read this exercise during the day, be still for a moment. When you are still, follow your breath, "in" and "out" as your abdomen rises and falls with your breath. Follow your breath through several cycles. Be at peace.

At the end of the day write in your journal one example of using this or any exercise to achieve a shift in perception that brought with it peace of mind. Remember your Disruptions Notebook.

MY STORY AND MY SCRIPTS
DISRUPT MY PEACE OF MIND.

Now is the time to look over your Disruptions Notebook. Here is how I would suggest doing that. Divide a page into four quadrants. Write "Men in Authority" in upper left quadrant. Write "Women in Authority" in the upper right quadrant. The lower left quadrant is for "Men Not in Authority," and the lower right quadrant is for "Women Not in Authority."

Flip through your Disruptions Notebook and write in each quadrant the personality characteristics describing each disruptive person in your stories of disruptions. Suppose that after doing that you have in your upper left quadrant the following characteristics: Inconsistent, picky, unreliable, faultfinding, blaming, drinks too much, fun at times, mood changes rapidly, gambling with other people's resources. Then ask yourself who in your childhood these characteristics would describe. Let's suppose that almost all of the characteristics at one time or another described your father, except "picky" and "gambling with other people's resources." Whom do these characteristics bring to mind? Maybe your grandfather, an uncle, or a friend of your father's whom you did not like. Suppose "picky" describes a friend of your father's you did not like and "gambling with other people's resources" reminds you of an uncle. You now have a picture of three characters in your story whom you will find over and over again. The strength of their influence will be diminished as you heal these relationships through forgiveness. Do this with each quadrant.

The persons these characteristics describe may surprise you. One person in an Attitudinal Healing group at the hospital found that the person most described in the upper left quadrant was his mother. He was recreating his conflicts with his mother in his disputes with the men in his life. This realization came to him rather dramatically one day when another driver, a man, cut his tractor-trailer off at a truck stop. Our group member jumped out of his truck and walked up to the man sitting in his car. "When he looked at me, I saw my mother's face." He went on to say that he knew he was overreacting, and for the first time in years turned away from a dramatic confrontation. "I said to myself, 'I could have peace instead of this'"

In another section entitled "Recurrent Fears" write the fears that come up over and over in your stories, such as: (1) Just when I achieve something I've been working for, everything will be taken away from me; (2) I will not find someone with whom I can form a lasting, loving relationship; (3) Close friends will turn on me.

Review this section each time you go through the lessons and a richer picture of the characters in your story will emerge. As you read the characteristics of the persons in your stories and your recurrent fears, incidents from childhood may reemerge. Describe these in a third section, "Childhood Memories." These three sections will catalogue the story you automatically bring forward from childhood to disrupt your adult experience. Just by putting these details down on paper you will begin to recognize them as they emerge again and again in your daily life. If you need some help processing these details, this is a good time to seek some psychotherapy or psychoanalysis from a qualified person in your community. If you do not know how to find such a person, there are some hints in the following chapter on "Afterwards." If you need more help than that, E-mail me and I will help.

When you are ready, begin formal meditation. First find a comfortable straight back chair. Sit erect in the chair with both feet planted on the floor. Put your hands on your legs or fold them in your lap. Close your eyes and notice your abdomen expand as you say "in" and contract as you say "out." Feel at peace as you follow your breath.

At the very end of the meditation see clearly in your mind the picture of your goal, in addition to peace of mind, for these eight weeks. Hold that picture. Notice the details. Feel at peace with that picture.

After meditation write this exercise on a card: *My story and my scripts disrupt my peace of mind.* Tonight write in your journal an example of using this or any exercise.

FORGIVENESS PAVES THE
ROAD TO PEACE.[72]

Remember that forgiving is not condoning. It is also not reconciliation. Reconciliation is an action. Forgiving is something I do in my mind. It is mostly a help to me, because it reduces my burden of resentment. Forgiveness is an opposite of blame.

My Aunt Betty is the best forgiver I know. No matter when I call her, it's just the right time. If I am late for dinner, it is fortuitous, because that pesky old roast took forever to cook. She treats my sister Barbara and me with kindness and forgiveness, no matter what. Aunt Betty is the epitome of inner peace.

I asked her once how she managed to be so forgiving. She told me, "Practice and determination." Before that I had not considered how much emotional strength it takes to hold your point of view despite the actions of others. I have enormous respect for Aunt Betty who was a background force of harmony throughout my childhood. If there was a need for help, Aunt Betty would come to lend a hand. She was there whenever we needed her. If I had been able to copy Aunt Betty when Renée left that Monday morning with my car keys, after my storm of pique had passed I would have said to myself, "Ah, an opportunity to walk to work and mindfully do some paper work there." Wouldn't that be great?

At the beginning and end of formal meditation repeat this exercise over several breath cycles: *Forgiveness paves the road to peace.*

When you are ready, begin formal meditation. Sit

comfortably erect in your straight back chair with both feet planted on the floor. Put your hands on your legs or fold them in your lap. Close your eyes and notice your abdomen expand as you say "in" and contract as you say "out." Feel at peace as you follow your breath.

1. After meditation write this exercise on a card or piece of paper that you will look at several times today: *Forgiveness paves the road to peace*. If you should feel blame at any time today, be still for a moment, and look at the exercise. Focus on the moment. Let yourself feel blame but when the feeling passes, let forgiveness reign. Each time you do, feel peace return.

At the end of the day write in your journal one example of using this or any exercise to achieve a shift in perception that brought with it peace of mind. Remember your Disruptions Notebook.

2. In the last few minutes of formal meditation imagine something that you may encounter in your life today that might stimulate blame in you. Feel the blame and when the storm of feeling passes think of the exercise today: *Forgiveness paves the road to peace*. Open yourself to forgiveness.

At the very end of the meditation see clearly in your mind the picture of your goal, in addition to peace of mind, for these eight weeks. Hold that picture. Notice the details. Feel at peace with that picture.

After meditation write this exercise on a card or piece of paper that you will look at several times today: *Forgiveness paves the road to peace*. Be still for a moment each time you read the exercise. When you are still, follow your breath, "in" and "out" as your abdomen rises and falls with your breath. Follow your breath through several cycles. Be at peace.

At the end of the day write in your journal one example of using this or any exercise to achieve a shift in perception that brought with it peace of mind. Remember your Disruptions Notebook.

3. In the last few minutes of formal meditation think back to a time in your past when you felt like blaming someone. Reexperience those feelings. When they pass, forgive.

When you are ready, let the white light build within you, fill you, and warm you. Let yourself and the other person be warmed by your bright light of love.

At the very end of the meditation see clearly in your mind the picture of your goal, in addition to peace of mind, for these eight weeks. Hold that picture. Notice the details. Feel at peace with that picture.

After meditation write this exercise on a card or piece of paper that you will look at several times today: *Forgiveness paves the road to peace*. Be still when you read the exercise. When you are still, follow your breath, "in" and "out" as your abdomen rises and falls with your breath. Follow your breath through several cycles. Be at peace.

At the end of the day write in your journal one example of using this or any exercise to achieve a shift in perception that brought with it peace of mind. Remember your Disruptions Notebook.

Exercise 5

HEALING IS MY CHOICE TO MAKE.[73]

Just as Aunt Betty said, practice and determination are what I need to make a choice for healing. One of the reasons to record a small instance of using a lesson each day is that if you get good at the little choices, you will slowly get better at the bigger ones.

Recently we had house guests for a weekend. I had been in charge of making the shopping list for breakfast food. Usually when we have guests, we make a breakfast buffet of cereal and fruits, but this time we decided that I would make omelets. However, when I opened the refrigerator, there were no eggs. I immediately became indignant. I knew I had put eggs on the shopping list, yet there were no eggs and our guests were about to come down for breakfast. I felt irritated. Then I stepped back, asked for guidance, and asked myself, "Do I want to be right or do I want peace of mind?" It was an easy choice. I put out fruit and cereal, just as we always did and it turned out fine. It seems like a little thing, but that is what life is made up of: little things that I can choose to turn into crises or moments of peace. The choice is mine.

At the beginning and end of formal meditation repeat this exercise over several breath cycles: *Healing is my choice to make.*

When you are ready begin formal meditation. First find a comfortable straight back chair. Sit erect in the chair with both feet planted on the floor. Put your hands on your legs or fold them in your lap. Close your eyes and notice your abdomen expand as you say "in" and contract as you say "out." Feel at peace as you follow your breath.

1. After meditation write this exercise on a card or piece of paper that you will look at several times today: *Healing is my choice to make*. If you should feel blame at any time today, be still for a moment, and look at the exercise. Focus on the moment. Let yourself feel blame, but when the feeling passes, let healing take place. Each time you do, feel peace return.

At the end of the day write in your journal one example of using this or any exercise to achieve a shift in perception that brought with it peace of mind. Remember your Disruptions Notebook.

2. In the last few minutes of formal meditation imagine something that you may encounter in your life today that might stimulate blame in you. Feel the blame, but when the storm of feelings passes, think of the lesson today: *Healing is my choice to make*. Open yourself to forgiveness.

At the very end of the meditation see clearly in your mind the picture of your goal, in addition to peace of mind, for these eight weeks. Hold that picture. Notice the details. Feel at peace with that picture.

After meditation write this exercise on a card or piece of paper that you will look at several times today: *Healing is my choice to make*. Be still each time you read the exercise today. When you are still, follow your breath, "in" and "out" as your abdomen rises and falls with your breath. Follow your breath through several cycles. Be at peace.

At the end of the day write in your journal one example of using this or any exercise to achieve a shift in perception that brought with it peace of mind. Remember your Disruptions Notebook.

3. In the last few minutes of formal meditation think back to a time in your past when you felt like blaming someone. Experience the feelings. When the storm of feelings passes, heal that wound with forgiveness.

When you are ready, let the white light build within your heart. Let it fill you and warm you. When you feel ready to share your kindness and compassion, allow the other person and yourself to be warmed by your bright light of love.

At the very end of the meditation see clearly in your mind the picture of your goal, in addition to peace of mind, for these eight weeks. Hold that picture. Notice the details. Feel at peace with that picture.

After meditation write this exercise on a card or piece of paper that you will look at several times today: *Healing is my choice to make*. Take a mini-break each time you read your exercise today. When you are still, follow your breath, "in" and "out" as your abdomen rises and falls with your breath. Follow your breath through several cycles. Be at peace.

At the end of the day write in your journal one example of using this or any exercise to achieve a shift in perception that brought with it peace of mind. Remember your Disruptions Notebook.

WE ARE STUDENTS AND TEACHERS
FOR EACH OTHER.[74]

Today after I came home from work there was a moment when Renée, Sam, Sarah and I were sitting in the barkatorium. There were no squirrels invading our yard, no dogs walking their owners past our house, and no menacing militant microbes, the invaders only Sam and Sarah can see. The rain was falling gently, and Sam and Sarah were in their meditation mode, eyes closed and curled up on either side of me on the sofa. Renée was reading in an easy chair. I looked at each of them and saw my teachers and my students. The three peaceful people in my house were teaching me how to take it easy and I was teaching them how successful they were as teachers. I enjoyed the moment.

At the beginning and end of formal meditation repeat this exercise over several breath cycles: *We are students and teachers for each other.*

When you are ready, begin formal meditation. Sit comfortably erect in your straight back chair with both feet planted on the floor. Put your hands on your legs or fold them in your lap. Close your eyes and notice your abdomen expand as you say "in" and contract as you say "out." Feel at peace as you follow your breath.

1. After meditation write this exercise on a card or piece of paper that you will look at several times today: *We are students and teachers for each other.* As you focus on the exercise, look around you. See the people clearly. Imagine what you are learning from them and what you are teaching them. Focus on the moment. Each time you do, feel peace.

At the end of the day write in your journal one example of using this or any exercise to achieve a shift in perception that brought with it peace of mind. Remember your Disruptions Notebook.

2. In the last few minutes of formal meditation imagine someone you may encounter today who has been a teacher to you. Remember the exercise: *We are students and teachers for each other*. Feel gratitude to your teacher.

At the very end of the meditation see clearly in your mind the picture of your goal, in addition to peace of mind, for these eight weeks. Hold that picture. Notice the details. Feel at peace with that picture.

After meditation write this exercise on a card or piece of paper that you will look at several times today: *We are students and teachers for each other*. During the day when you read your exercise, be still for a moment. When you are still, follow your breath, "in" and "out" as your abdomen rises and falls through several cycles. Be at peace.

At the end of the day write in your journal one example of using this or any exercise to achieve a shift in perception that brought with it peace of mind. Remember your Disruptions Notebook.

3. In the last few minutes of formal meditation think back to a time when you experienced someone as an important teacher. Imagine what that person may have learned from you. Feel gratitude.

When you are ready, let the white light build within your heart. Let it fill you and warm you. When you feel ready to share your light, let yourself and the other person be warmed by your bright light of love.

At the very end of the meditation see clearly in your mind the picture of your goal, in addition to peace of mind, for these eight weeks. Hold that picture. Notice the details. Feel at peace with that picture.

After meditation write this exercise on a card or piece of paper that you will look at several times today: *We are students and teachers for each other*. During the day when you read the exercise, be still for a moment. When you are still, follow your breath, "in" and "out" as your abdomen rises and falls with your breath. Follow your breath through several cycles. Be at peace.

At the end of the day write in your journal one example of using this or any exercise to achieve a shift in perception that brought with it peace of mind. Remember your Disruptions Notebook.

I WILL GIVE UP CONTROL AND
TRUST THE FORCE.[75]

I know of no greater gift than to have confidence in this lesson. When I am without a clue about what to do I say to myself, "I will step back and trust the force." I may say to others who are looking to me for guidance, "Let's see how the spirit moves us." It is amazing how readily my colleagues and friends accept this guidance. If you get only one thing from this course—the confidence that you can always find a way by stepping back and trusting your inner wisdom—you will have attained all I could ever hope to teach you.

If you would like to use this capacity even more efficiently, it might be useful to add another goal for the second and third times through the lessons. One way to get in touch with goals is to use this formula. Think of goals as being either spiritual, psychological, material, or physical. Write down one of each. For example: Spiritual—I would like to develop a reverent attitude toward other people. Psychological—I would like to stop reacting defensively when I experience criticism. Material—I would like to pay off my VISA card. Physical—I would like to lose five pounds.

Choose one to pursue in the next eight weeks. Now imagine, in as much detail as possible, one of these goals. Imagine being a calm, reverent person in the midst of a sarcastic, ironic group. Or, imagine a person who usually goads you successfully, surprised when suddenly met with respectful non-defensiveness. Or, imagine all zeros on your VISA bill. Or, see yourself in the mirror five pounds lighter. See the picture of your goal clearly in your mind. Repeat this picture to yourself at the end of each daily meditation in the next eight weeks.

At the beginning and end of formal meditation repeat this exercise over several breath cycles: *I will give up control and trust the force.*

When you are ready, begin formal meditation.

1. After meditation write this exercise on a card or piece of paper that you will look at several times today: *I will give up control and trust the force.* Each time you do, feel peace and inspiration.

At the end of the day write in your journal one example of using this or any exercise to achieve a shift in perception that brought with it peace of mind. Remember your Disruptions Notebook.

2. In the last few minutes of formal meditation imagine someone you may encounter today who is likely to pose a problem that you will not be able to answer. Remember the exercise: *I will give up control and trust the force.* Imagine your trusting this inner wisdom.

At the very end of the meditation see clearly in your mind the picture of your goal, in addition to peace of mind, for these eight weeks. Hold that picture. Notice the details. Feel at peace with that picture.

After meditation write this exercise on a card or piece of paper that you will look at several times today: *I will give up control and trust the force.* During the day be still when you read your exercise. When you are still, follow your breath, "in" and "out" as your abdomen rises and falls with your breath. Follow your breath through several cycles. Be at peace.

At the end of the day describe an instance when you dealt with blame effectively by using this or any exercise. Remember your Disruptions Notebook.

3. In the last few minutes of formal meditation think back to a time in your past when you experienced a person who inspired you to trust yourself.

Feel gratitude to this person who has been a model for you. Two close friends, Charles Bingham and Charles Ricker, were models for me. Remember that you do not have to have answers, just a feeling of confidence that answers will come if you trust the force.

When you are ready, let the white light build within your heart, fill you, and warm you. Let yourself and the other person be warmed by your bright light of love.

You may say, "Oh sure, getting in touch with bright warm light must be easy for you. After all, the worst thing that ever happened to you would make an amusing *Ozzie and Harriet* program."

It may seem from the stories in this book that my biggest trauma was not being able to assemble a model airplane. I assure you that is not so. I have kept the stories in a lighter vein on purpose. It is not possible to go through life without suffering the death of a loved one, abuse from a caregiver, betrayal by a trusted one, rejection by a significant person, and other forms of more serious trauma. Many psychoanalysts have suffered very major trauma. It is one of the things that attracts us to our work. We teach what we hope to learn.

I chose the incidents in this book to reveal something, but not to burden my patients, my loved ones, and myself too much. It is important that my psychoanalytic patients be able to speak freely about whatever comes into their minds. If they were to know too much about my traumas, they might be reluctant to tell me about theirs for fear of upsetting me.

At the very end of the meditation see clearly in your mind the picture of your goal, in addition to peace of mind, for these eight weeks. Hold that picture. Notice the details. Feel at peace with that picture.

After meditation write this exercise on a card or piece of paper that you will look at several times today: *I will give up control and trust the force.*

At the end of the day write in your journal one example of using this or any exercise to achieve a shift in perception that brought with it peace of mind. Remember your Disruptions Notebook.

Part III
Afterwards

This course is designed to help you begin a journey of lifelong learning. Here are some suggested routes of study:

ATTITUDINAL HEALING

After you have been through these exercises three times, most of their important elements will be stored in your unconscious mind. You can continue to use one exercise a day indefinitely. In addition, you may decide to join an Attitudinal Healing group in your area. For information on the location of the group nearest you, call the Network for Attitudinal Healing International at (512) 327-4568. The books by Gerald Jampolsky on Attitudinal Healing are available through The Miracle Distribution Center at (714) 738-8380. My personal favorites are *Love is Letting Go of Fear* and *Love is the Answer*.

A COURSE IN MIRACLES®

Another route is to read *A Course in Miracles*® and find a study group in your area. A study group is almost essential because of the difficulties routinely encountered in reading this work. To find the nearest study group, call the Miracle Distribution Center at (714) 738-8380 and ask to be put on their mailing list. They offer a wealth of books on the subject of healing.

An excellent explanatory work is *A Return to Love* by Marianne Williamson (New York: HarperCollins, 1992). She also explains the metaphors in *A Course in Miracles*. Implementing the lessons and text is much easier if you do not get stuck in some of the metaphorical language.

MINDFULNESS MEDITATION

Mindfulness Meditation is a direction that easily dovetails with a study of Attitudinal Healing. In fact, the principles of Attitudinal Healing may be thought of as bite-sized pieces of philosophy that make Mindfulness Meditation more easily useable. Other excellent books on meditation are:

Hanh, Thich Nhat. *The Miracle of Mindfulness: A Manual of Meditation*. Boston: Beacon Press, 1976.
Kabat-Zinn, Jon. *Wherever You Go, There You Are*. New York: Hyperion, 1994.
Kornfield, Jack. *A Path With Heart*. New York: Bantam Books, 1993.

SELECTING EXERCISES FROM ANY BOOK

Of all these books, only *A Course in Miracles* has a work-book, but you can turn any book into a workbook in this manner. Read a few pages each morning. Make it a range of pages rather than a fixed number. I usually read from one to five pages each morning. I use a highlighter to emphasize the most important points. When I finish my reading, I go back and choose a thought that I would like to be my exercise for the day. I write that thought in the margin of the book with a pencil. I use that thought just like the exercises in this workbook; then I meditate. After meditation I write the exercise on a card that I carry in a frequently used pocket. When it is convenient I pull out the exercise and am still for a minute or so. In this man-ner, any book can be a workbook, and you, too, can enjoy the rewards of life-long meditation and learning.

Journaling a success each day and any serious dis-ruptions is still a good idea no matter which book you read.

PSYCHOANALYSIS

If you are interested in learning more about your story and how that influences you throughout your daily life, you may wish to try psychoanalysis. In many major cities there are psychoanalysts who will see patients for a range of fees. People who want psychoanalysis can find it at a price they can afford after an assessment to make sure that it is the optimal treatment. The American Psychoanalytic Association has a number of institutes and training facili-ties around the country. In addition, there are Division

39 Institutes sponsored by The American Psychological Association, Institutes of The International Psychoanalytic Association and independent institutes sponsored by universities, such as New York University. There is no centralized phone number for these Institutes but the Yellow Pages often includes local listings. Many institutes have a psychotherapy program for those who want to start out more slowly at first before trying psychoanalysis.

Psychoanalysis is conducted with the patient lying on a couch. Psychotherapy is conducted face to face. Psychotherapy is conducted with one or two visits per week. Psychoanalysis is conducted with more visits per week. The conduct of the therapist is similar whether the patient is in psychoanalysis or psychotherapy. The major difference is in what comes to the mind of the patient. In both psychotherapy and psychoanalysis the patient tries to say whatever comes into his or her mind. Lying on the couch in psychoanalysis allows more to come to mind, and more frequent sessions permit a more cohesive investigation.

Here is the number of the American Psychoanalytic Association to help you find the nearest resource in your area: (212) 752-0450.

An interesting integrative work is *Contemporary Psychoanalysis and Eastern Thought* by John R. Suler, Albany, NY: State University of New York Press, 1993.

JOURNALING

The best book with more about journaling is *At a Journal Workshop* by Ira Progoff, Ph.D., Los Angeles: Jeremy P. Tarcher, 1975, 1992. I am indebted to Jim Boeglin for giving me this book. It has an excellent section on "Spiritual Steppingstones" and "Inner Wisdom Dialogue" that is a perfect fit with meditation study.

OPRAH

Watch Oprah. Oprah Winfrey has a commitment to healing. Often she visits with authors who share that commitment such as Marianne Williamson, Deepak Chopra, and Dean Ornish. Those of you, like me, who are never at home when her program is on the air might form an Oprah taping consortium. We have an informal agreement in our Monday Attitudinal Healing group to share tapes of her programs that spotlight these authors.

BRIAN LAMB

Watch Brian Lamb on C-Span. "Call-In," "Journalists' Round Table," and "Booknotes" give optimal exposure to Mr. Lamb's defenseless neutrality as well as his balanced appreciation of the day's important issues. His neutrality is something that we could all imitate.

HOW PSYCHOTHERAPISTS MIGHT USE THIS BOOK

At Columbia Hospital in Milwaukee, Attitudinal Healing is the basis for many of our Behavioral Medicine programs. In individual psychotherapy we encourage patients to start the program in this book and to talk to us each session about the successes or the trouble they experience in implementing any exercise. We suggest that when an exercise is difficult, they try it one day and then move on to the next. Some patients prefer to stay with the difficult exercise until they master it. We prefer that they move on, because the key to using the exercises is repetition. When the exercises are repeated, their connection becomes apparent and they all merge into one. An exercise that is hard to use the first time through the book will be easier after going through all the exercises once. The beginning exercises are the most difficult to implement. We tell our patients this and urge them not to become discouraged.

In addition to individual therapy we offer a weekly group in which participants share their successes in using the lessons. Before being admitted to the group each participant is required to attend a three-hour introductory course that covers the material in this book prior to the exercises. In the introductory course we spend about half the time teaching meditation, including twenty minutes of meditation practice in the group.

In the weekly group we begin by identifying ourselves. Then we go around the group again and the participants may either pass or share a moment of healing. These groups are inspirational. Most of us leave with an increased resolve to use our exercises, do our meditation no matter what, journal our successes, and write down our disruptions. We limit group participation to sharing moments of healing, that is, successes. This makes the group a very safe place, because the members are protected from revealing details of failure that might embarrass them. Eventually, through sharing their successes they reveal the edges of their major concerns, but only in due time and as they feel safe in the group.

The second time around the group we focus on problems implementing particular exercises. Our interventions in this part of the group may include explanations of concepts as they relate to *A Course in Miracles*,® encouragement not to get bogged down in a momentary setback and move on to the next lesson, and/or sharing similar difficulties with an exercise and how we overcame that obstacle. Once a month we say something about how long we have been a student of Attitudinal Healing and *A Course in Miracles*® and what we have gained from it so far. We mix our participantsin all but one group, which is solely devoted to *A Course in Miracles*®. In most of our groups some of us are studying Attitudinal Healing and some are studying *A Course in Miracles*®. This has resulted in a healthy mix of participants who are eager to see different paths.

The third time around the group we focus on meditation and how each participant's practice is going. We encourage daily practice in mindfulness meditation whether it be sitting, walking, or exercising. We emphasize doing some sitting meditation daily, even for just a few minutes at first. As we progress we encourage increasing the daily time in meditation.

Occasionally we have participants who are so distracted by disruptions that they cannot use the groups or the exercises very well. Often these participants will not return after the three-hour introductory course, but if they do, the rest of us try to help them by our listening and our example. We encourage people who are distracted by disruptions to seek individual therapy, and we have a number of resources to offer them including the Behavioral Medicine Psychotherapy Clinic; a sliding fee scale, psychoanalytically oriented psychotherapy clinic; a reduced fee psychoanalysis clinic; and clinics for medication management. We offer introductory courses in Attitudinal Healing once a month. Every two months we offer introductory classes in meditation. We also offer classes in Tai Chi and Nutrition. We offer a public forum on *A Course in Miracles*® every three months. We offer one group weekly solely devoted to the study of *A Course in Miracles*®.

When instructing therapists who wish to use this text in psychotherapy I have found that forming a study group is the most important part of the program. Even if the group is small (two, three, or four to begin) it is the best way to experience reinforcement for the considerable effort required. Try to meet once a week for an hour. If you have done the first seven lessons, take turns sharing a successful application of each one until the time runs out. You may choose to begin and end by joining hands in a moment of peaceful silence. After your therapists' group has been through the lessons once, you may feel comfortable letting others join you. They do not have to be in the same place in the book. They can still participate in sharing a moment of healing when their turn comes. Keep the group focused mainly on sharing successes. Difficulties in using particular lessons can be saved until the last part of the session. It will keep the group a supportive place for all to learn from each other's successes. Take a few minutes at the end of the session to talk about each participant's meditation practice.

If any therapist wishes to ask specific questions about using this book in psychotherapy, please feel free to write me at America On Line at TodDav or Internet at TodDav @ aol.com or 2015 East Newport Avenue, Milwaukee, WI 53211-2949.

LEND ME YOUR EXAMPLES

If you are using this book, I would appreciate hearing from you. Please send me any example of your success with a specific lesson. I am interested in hearing about even the smallest example. I would like to compile a book of these examples crediting them to those of you who are kind enough to share them with me. Please write me at America On Line at TodDav or Internet at TodDav @ aol.com or Todd Davison, M.D., 2015 East Newport Avenue, 801, Milwaukee, WI 53211-2949.

Notes

1. The term *Attitudinal Healing* was coined by Judith Skutch Whitson when meditating with Gerald Jampolsky, according to Susan S. Trout, Ph.D., in her book *To See Differently*, Three Roses Press, Washington, DC, 1990, p. 25. Dr. Jampolsky is the founder of the Attitudinal Healing movement.
2. *A Course in Miracles®* is a registered trademark and servicemark of the Foundation for Inner Peace. All paraphrasing of the principles of Attitudinal Healing that derive from the *Course* are the personal interpretation of the author and are not necessarily endorsed by the copyright holder of *A Course in Miracles®*. 3. Unless otherwise specified all footnotes refer to *A Course in Miracles®*, Foundation for Inner Peace, P.O. Box 598, Mill Valley, CA 94942, 1975. This footnote refers to a direct quote of the Workbook (abbreviated: W-, henceforth; as Text is abbreviated T-; and Teachers Manual is abbreviated M-.) "I could see peace instead of this," W-51. 4. This idea stems from "I see nothing as it is now." W-15. 5. Emotions may be viewed as either love or fear is a paraphrase of "You have but two emotions, love and

fear." T-230. *6.* This is a paraphrase of "Forgiveness is the key to happiness." W-214. *7.* This idea stems from "Heaven is the decision I must make." W-264. *8.* This idea stems from a discussion on T-99–100. *9.* This idea stems from "In quiet I receive God's Word today." W-225. *10.* This is the same as endnote #4 above. *11.* This is the same as endnote #5 above. *12.* This idea is explored in T-294–297. *13.* This is the same as endnote #6 above. *14.* This is the same as endnote #7 above. *15.* This is the same as endnote #8 above. *16.* This is the same as endnote #9 above. *17.* These ideas stem from the lesson titles "I am determined to see things differently," and "There is another way to see the world," found in W-32 and W-50. *18.* This is the same as endnote #5 above. *19.* This is the same as endnote #4 above. *20.* This is the same as endnote #4 above. *21.* This idea stems from the lesson "I am never upset for the reason I think," on W-8. *22.* This idea stems from the lesson "I do not know what anything is for," on W-38. *23.* This idea stems from the lesson "I have given everything I see all the meaning that it has for me," on W-4. *24.* This idea stems from the lesson "I have invented the world I see," found on W-49. *25. Love is the Answer* by Gerald G. Jampolsky, M.D., and Diane V. Cirincione. New York: Bantam Books, 1991, p. 37. *26.* This idea stems from the lesson "I do not perceive my own best interests." W-36. *27.* This is the same as endnote #4 above. *28.* This is the same as endnote #5 above. *29.* This is the same as endnote #5 above. *30.* This idea stems from the lesson "My grievances hid the light of the world in me," found on W-117. *31.* This idea is drawn from many places in the *Course*. It is most clearly reflected in the heading "Is My Communication in this Relationship for Joining or Separation?" in *Love Is The Answer* by Gerald G. Jampolsky, M.D., and Diane V. Cirincione, p. 74. *32. Change Your Mind, Change Your Life*, by Gerald G. Jampolsky, M.D., and Diane V. Cirincione. New York: Bantam, 1993, p. 13. *33.* This idea stems from the lesson "I can escape from the world I see by giving up attack thoughts," on W-34. *34.* This idea stems in part from the lesson "Only my condemnation injures me," on W-379. *35.* This exercise is a paraphrase from this sentence in *Love Is Letting Go Of Fear* by Gerald G. Jampolsky and Diane V. Cirincione. New York: Bantam Books, 1991, p. 70. "We begin to truly establish loving rela-

tionships when we commit ourselves to listening with love."
36. This is paraphrased from "Do I want to be happy or do I want
to be right?" in *Love Is The Answer* by Gerald G. Jampolsky,
M.D., and Diane V. Cirincione, p. 109. *37.* This exercise is based
in part on the lesson "I see only the past." W-11. *38.* This lesson
is paraphrased from "Today I choose to tear up my scripts for
other people," in *Love Is The Answer* by Gerald G. Jampolsky
and Diane V. Cirincione, p. 181. *39.* This exercise is based on "I
am not a victim of the world I see," from W-48. *40.* This exercise is a paraphrase of the lesson "Whatever suffers is not a part
of me," W-417. *41.* This exercise is based on "Attachments: the
jailor within" from *Love Is The Answer* by Gerald G. Jampolsky,
M.D., and Diane V. Cirincione, pp. 105–115. *42.* This idea stems
from "This day I choose to spend in perfect peace," W-422.
43. Free to Choose by Milton and Rose Friedman, New York and
London: Hartcourt, Brace and Jovanovich, 1980, p. 2. *44.* This
is a repeat of endnote #6 above. *45.* This idea stems from "I will
find no value in blaming myself or others." It is found in *Love Is
The Answer* on page 161. *46.* This exercise is based on the same
quote as the one in endnote #45. *47.* Thich Nhat Hanh, *The
Miracle of Mindfulness: A Manual of Meditation.* Boston: Beacon Press, 1976, p. 22. *48.* This exercise is based on the lesson
"I could see peace instead of this," W-51. *49.* This is the same as
endnote #7 above. *50.* This exercise is based on Chapter 1, "The
meaning of miracles," T-3–16. *51.* This exercise is based on the
same material as in endnote #50 above. *52.* This exercise is based
on the same material as in endnote #50 above. *53.* This exercise is based on "This is my holy instant of release," W-405.
54. This exercise is based on "I will step back and let Him lead
the way," W-291. *55.* This exercise is based on "When I am healed
I am not healed alone." W-261. *56.* This is the same as endnote
#8. *57.* This is the ninth principle of Attitudinal Healing as found
on page 14 of *Change Your Mind, Change Your Life.* *58.* This is
based on the line in Lesson 296, "We teach today what we would
learn." W-446. *59. Change Your Mind, Change Your Life,* p. 25.
60. This idea is based on "All things are lessons God would have
me learn," W-357. *61.* This exercise is based on "Be You in
charge. For I would follow You, certain that Your direction gives
me peace," W-486. *62.* This is the same as endnote #9. *63.* This

idea is based on "In quiet I receive God's word today." W-220. *64.* This idea is based on "Fear is not justified in any form." W-402. *65.* This exercise is based on "The Holy Spirit looks through me today." W-446. *66.* This exercise is based on "In the quiet I receive God's word today." W-225. *67.* This is based on "I place my future in the hands of God." W-360. *68.* This idea is based on "I will step back and let Him lead the way." W-284. *69.* This is the same as endnote #4 above. *70.* This is based on the citation in endnote #4 plus that in endnote #26 above. *71.* This is the same as endnote #5 above. *72.* This is the same as endnote #6 above. *73.* This is the same as endnote #7 above. *74.* This is the same as endnote #57 above. *75.* This is based on "I will step back and let Him lead the way." W-291.

Index